RHINE
RIVER CRUISE
TRAVEL GUIDE
2024 EDITION

"Capturing Rhine's Essence: A Symphony of Scenic Marvels, Culture, and Timeless Elegance"

Jack X. Woodburn

Copyright © 2024 Jack X. Woodburn

All Rights Reserved

All rights reserved. No part of this book may be reproduced, stored, or transmitted in any form or by any means, electronic, mechanical, photocopying, recording, scanning, or otherwise, without prior written permission from the publisher.

Table of contents

IMPORTANT NOTE 7
BEFORE READING 7
Introduction 9
    WELCOME ABOARD 9
    WHY CHOOSE A RHINE RIVER CRUISE? 10
    HOW TO SETTING SAIL ON THE RHINE 12
    IMPORTANCE OF RHINE RIVER CRUISES 15
Chapter One 20
PLANNING YOUR RHINE ADVENTURE 20
    CHOOSING THE RIGHT CRUISE PACKAGE 20
    BEST TIME TO VISIT THE RHINE RIVER 23
    DURATION OF THE CRUISE 25
    VISA AND DOCUMENTATION 27
    BOOKING TIPS AND DISCOUNTS 30
Chapter Two 34
RHINE RIVER ESSENTIALS 34
    GEOGRAPHY AND TOPOGRAPHY 34
NAVIGATING THE RHINE: PORTS AND ITINERARY OPTIONS .. 36
    Amsterdam: The Gateway to Your Rhine Adventure 36
    Strasbourg: A Blend of French and German Flair 39
    The Romantic Rhine: Castles, Vineyards, and Fairytale Villages 41
    Cologne: A Tale of Cathedrals and Culture 43
    Basel: Where the Rhine Journey Concludes 45
    PACKING TIPS AND ESSENTIALS 47
Chapter Three 52
EMBARKING ON THE RHINE JOURNEY 52
    DEPARTURE PORTS AND EMBARKATION PROCEDURES ... 52
    THE RIVER CRUISE SHIP EXPERIENCE 55

YOUR STATEROOM: A HOME ON THE WATER 57
Chapter Four..**62**
RHINE RIVER REGIONS AND DESTINATIONS............**62**
   UPPER RHINE: BASEL TO STRASBOURG 62
   MIDDLE RHINE: KOBLENZ TO MAINZ.....................65
   LOWER RHINE: DUSSELDORF TO AMSTERDAM 69
   SIDE EXCURSIONS: OFF THE BEATEN PATH............72
Chapter Five **76**
HISTORIC LANDMARKS ALONG THE RHINE **76**
   UNESCO WORLD HERITAGE SITES.......................76
      Cologne Cathedral (Cologne, Germany)......................76
      Rhine Gorge (Germany)...79
      Strasbourg- Grande le (Strasbourg, France)...............82
      Speyer Cathedral (Speyer, Germany)........................85
      Kinderdijk-Elshout (Alblasserwaard, Netherlands)..............87
      Historic Monuments of Ancient Cologne (Cologne, Germany).90
      Upper Middle Rhine Valley_(Germany).......................93
   ICONIC CASTLES AND FORTRESSES 95
      Marksburg Castle: A Timeless Fortress 95
      Rheinstein Castle: Where Romance Meets Architecture 98
      Burg Eltz: A Fairytale in the Eifel Forest....................100
      Cochem Castle: A Crown Above the Moselle 103
      Ehrenbreitstein Fortress: Guardian of Koblenz 106
   CHARMING RIVERSIDE TOWNS 108
      Rüdesheim am Rhein: A Winemaker's Paradise............108
      COCHEM: A FAIRYTALE BY THE MOSELLE 111
      Bacharach: Where History Meets Riverside Tranquility 114
      COLMAR: ALSATIAN ELEGANCE ON THE RHINE 116
      Koblenz: The Confluence of History and Modernity............118
      Heidelberg: Scholarly Splendor on the River Neckar 120
   VISITING CHARMING VILLAGES 122
      Zons: A Living Medieval Town 122

{3}

    Bacharach: A Medieval Jewel 124
    Assmannshausen: A Wine Lover's Haven 126
    Rüdesheim: Where Wine and Tradition Meet 129
    Cochem: Fairytale Setting on the Moselle River 131

Chapter Six 134
SCENIC BEAUTY 134
BREATHTAKING LANDSCAPES..134
FLORA AND FAUNA OF THE RHINE VALLEY 136
PHOTOGRAPHY TIPS FOR CAPTURING THE BEAUTY 138
NATURE RESERVES AND WILDLIFE....................................141
Nature Reserves Along the Rhine 141
The Rhine Gorge: A Natural Wonderland 144
Conservation Efforts and Sustainable Tourism................148
Seasonal Highlights in Wildlife 151
Chapter Seven 156
CULTURAL IMMERSION 156
    LOCAL CUSTOMS AND TRADITIONS 156
    GREETINGS AND POLITENESS 159
    Festivals and Celebrations 161
    Wine Culture..164
    Dining Etiquette 166
    Religious Customs 169
    Folklore and Superstitions 173
    Arts and Crafts 176
CULINARY DELIGHTS OF THE RHINE 179
    Cologne's Culinary Palette 179
    Local Delicacies in Amsterdam 181
    Romantic Rhine: Vineyards and Gastronomy 183
    Strasbourg's Fusion of French and German Influences 185
    DINING ABOARD THE CRUISE SHIP 187
Chapter Eight..192
ACTIVITIES AND EXCURSIONS 192

GUIDED TOURS AND SHORE EXCURSIONS 192
   Exploring Cultural Gems: 192
   Castle Adventures: 195
   Culinary Expeditions: 198
   Scenic Walks and Nature Escapes: 201
   CUSTOMIZING YOUR EXPERIENCE: 204
   Recommended Guided Tours And Shore Excursions Company 207
OUTDOOR ADVENTURES ALONG THE RHINE 209
RELAXATION AND WELLNESS OPTIONS 213

Chapter Nine **218**
ONBOARD EXPERIENCE **218**
TYPES OF RHINE RIVER CRUISE SHIPS 218
   Longships: A Blend of Innovation and Tradition 218
   Riverboats: Navigating Elegance 222
   Boutique Cruises: Personalized Intimacy 225
   Luxury Cruises: Opulence on the Water 229
CABIN SELECTION AND AMENITIES 232
DINING AND ENTERTAINMENT 236

Chapter Ten **242**
PRACTICAL TIPS FOR RHINE RIVER TRAVEL **242**
TRANSPORTATION TO AND FROM PORTS 242
   Air Travel Considerations 242
   Pre-Cruise Transportation Planning 245
   Ground Transportation Options 248
   Self-Drive and Parking Facilities 254
EMERGENCY PROCEDURES 257
SAFETY AND HEALTH CONSIDERATIONS 261
INTERACTING WITH LOCALS: LANGUAGE AND ETIQUETTE 265
SOUVENIRS AND MEMENTOS 269

CONCLUSION **274**
FOND FAREWELL ON YOUR RHINE RIVER ADVENTURE ... 274

APPENDIX **279**
　Language Tips: Basic German Phrases...................................279

IMPORTANT NOTE
BEFORE READING

You might find a special trip experience in these pages.

The purpose of this Rhine river cruise guide is to inspire your creativity, imagina-tion, and sense of adventure.

Since we think that the beauty of every discovery should be experienced firsthand, free from visual filter and prejudices, you won't find any pictures here.

Every monument, every location, and every secret nook are waiting for you when you get there, eager to surprise and amaze you.

Why should we ruin the wonder and excitement of the initial impression? Prepare to set off on a voyage where your imagination will serve as both your single mode of transportation and your personal tour guide. Keep in mind that your own creations are the most attractive.

This book lacks a map and photographs, in contrast to many other manuals.

Why? Because in our opinion the best discoveries are made when a person gets lost, let themselves go with the flow of the environment, and embraces the ambiguity of the road.

Be cautious, trust your gut, and expect the unexpected. In a world without maps, where roads are made with each step you take, the magic of the voyage starts now.

Introduction

WELCOME ABOARD

Embarking on a Rhine River Cruise is a poetic sojourn through the heart of Europe, where the majestic Rhine River weaves a tale of history, culture, and natural beauty. As you step aboard, envision yourself drifting through landscapes straight from a fairy tale—medieval castles perched on vineyard-draped hills, charming villages with cobblestone streets, and panoramic vistas that unfold like chapters in a well-loved novel.

The allure of a Rhine River Cruise lies not just in the destinations it visits but in the unhurried rhythm of the journey. Picture yourself on the sun-drenched deck, a gentle breeze carrying the whispers of legends from lore-rich shores.

This is not a mere cruise; it's a curated experience, an odyssey that transcends the ordinary, inviting you to revel in the romance of Europe's most iconic waterway.

Join us as we navigate the currents of culture, savor the flavors of local cuisine, and create memories against the backdrop of centuries-old landmarks. Your Rhine River Cruise is more than a voyage; it's a symphony of moments, each note played by the landscapes, cultures, and stories that unfold along the way. Welcome aboard this floating masterpiece, where the enchantment of the Rhine awaits you at every turn.

WHY CHOOSE A RHINE RIVER CRUISE?

Embarking on a Rhine River Cruise is an exquisite choice, weaving together a tapestry of experiences that make it a voyage like no other. Let's explore the compelling reasons why choosing a Rhine River Cruise is not just a travel decision but an invitation to immerse yourself in the quintessence of European charm.

Captivating Scenery:

A Rhine River Cruise unfolds like a moving landscape painting. Imagine sailing through the picturesque Rhine Gorge, where vineyard-clad hills, medieval castles, and storybook villages create a panorama that transcends the ordinary.

Cultural Odyssey:

As the cruise glides along, you'll dock at historic cities and charming towns, each pulsating with its unique cultural heartbeat. From the iconic Cologne Cathedral to the medieval allure of Strasbourg, the Rhine's banks are adorned with treasures waiting to be explored.

Relaxed Exploration:

Unlike traditional land-based tours, a Rhine River Cruise allows you to unpack once and experience multiple destinations. Wake up each day in a new port, ready to explore without the hassle of constant packing and unpacking.

Luxurious Comfort:

The cruise ship becomes your floating sanctuary, where elegant cabins, gourmet dining, and onboard amenities ensure a luxurious retreat. It's not just about the destinations; it's about the journey being as enchanting as the ports of call.

Culinary Delights:

Indulge in a gastronomic journey as you savor local delicacies and world-class cuisine on board. Each meal is a celebration of the regions you traverse, offering a delightful fusion of flavors that mirror the diversity along the Rhine.

Historic Castles and Landmarks:

The Rhine is adorned with a necklace of castles, each with its own tale of chivalry and romance. Cruise past iconic landmarks like Marksburg Castle and Lorelei Rock, where the river echoes with the whispers of history.

Personalized Experiences:

Whether you prefer guided excursions, leisurely walks through charming towns, or immersing yourself in local markets, a Rhine River Cruise offers a range of activities to suit your preferences. It's your journey, curated to reflect your travel desires.

Timeless Romance:

The Rhine exudes a romantic aura, and a cruise along its waters is a celebration of love and connection. Whether you're sharing a quiet moment on the sundeck or exploring fairytale villages hand in hand, the Rhine sets the stage for timeless romance.

Choosing a Rhine River Cruise is an invitation to be part of a story—a story written in the melodies of flowing water, the rustle of vineyard leaves, and the echoes of centuries-old legends. It's a journey where every moment is an ode to the enchantment that only the Rhine can offer.

HOW TO SETTING SAIL ON THE RHINE

Setting sail on the Rhine is an exhilarating adventure that promises a blend of picturesque landscapes, historic cities, and cultural richness. Here's your guide on how to embark on this unforgettable journey:

Research and Choose Your Cruise:

- Begin by researching Rhine River cruise options. Consider factors such as cruise duration, itinerary, cruise line reputation, and onboard amenities.

- Choose a cruise that aligns with your interests, whether it's exploring historic castles, tasting local wines, or experiencing vibrant city life.

Selecting the Right Time:

- The Rhine is charming year-round, but certain times offer unique experiences. Spring and summer bring lush landscapes, while the fall foliage is a visual spectacle. Winter cruises often feature festive markets.

Booking Your Cruise:

- Once you've chosen the cruise that suits you, book your tickets well in advance. This ensures you secure your preferred cabin and embarkation dates.

Preparing Travel Documents:

- Check passport validity and visa requirements for the countries you'll visit. Ensure you have all necessary travel documents, including cruise confirmation, travel insurance, and any required visas.

Packing Essentials:

- Pack according to the season and activities. Comfortable walking shoes, layered clothing, and a camera for capturing the scenic beauty are must-haves. Many cruises have casual dress codes.

Embarkation Day:

- Arrive at the embarkation port with ample time. Complete check-in procedures, receive your cruise card, and settle into your cabin.

- Attend the mandatory safety briefing to familiarize yourself with onboard procedures.

Exploring the Ship:

- Familiarize yourself with the ship's layout. Discover common areas, dining venues, entertainment options, and any onboard activities.

- Take a moment to relax on the deck and soak in the anticipation of the journey ahead.

Participating in Onboard Activities:

- Rhine River cruises often feature onboard activities, such as lectures about the region, wine tastings, and cultural performances. Engage in these to enhance your understanding of the destinations.

Shore Excursions:

- Plan your shore excursions based on the itinerary. Whether it's exploring medieval castles, wandering through charming villages, or tasting local cuisine, make the most of the opportunities ashore.

Culinary Delights:

- Enjoy the diverse culinary offerings onboard. Rhine River cruises showcase regional dishes, and many cruises offer inclusive dining options.

Immerse in Local Culture:

- Embrace the local culture at each port of call. Engage with locals, try regional specialties, and explore historical sites to make your journey truly immersive.

Capturing Memories:

- Document your journey through photographs and journaling. The Rhine's landscapes and historic sites provide ample opportunities for creating lasting memories.

Disembarkation:

- On the final day, follow disembarkation procedures. Ensure all personal belongings are packed, settle any onboard expenses, and disembark with a heart full of memories.

IMPORTANCE OF RHINE RIVER CRUISES

Rhine River cruises hold significant importance, offering a unique and enriching travel experience that goes beyond the ordinary.

Scenic Beauty:

The Rhine River winds through breathtaking landscapes, showcasing vineyards, charming villages, and historic castles. Cruising along this iconic waterway provides passengers with unparalleled views of nature's beauty.

Cultural Richness:

The Rhine Valley is steeped in history and culture. Cruises often include stops at cities and towns with well-preserved architecture, allowing passengers to immerse themselves in the rich heritage of the region.

Historic Castles and Fortresses:

The Rhine is adorned with a multitude of medieval castles and fortresses, each with its own story to tell. Cruises offer the opportunity to explore these historic landmarks, offering a glimpse into the past.

Vibrant Cities:

Cruises along the Rhine often include visits to vibrant cities such as Cologne, Strasbourg, and Basel. Passengers can explore these urban centers, experiencing the blend of modern life and historical charm.

Wine Regions:

The Rhine Valley is renowned for its vineyards and wine production. Cruises take passengers through wine regions like the Moselle, allowing them to savor local wines and learn about the winemaking traditions.

Relaxing Journey:

Rhine River cruises provide a leisurely and relaxing mode of travel. Passengers can enjoy the picturesque scenery from the comfort of the ship, creating a serene and stress-free journey.

Culinary Delights:

Cruises often showcase the diverse culinary offerings of the Rhine Valley. Passengers can indulge in regional specialties, gourmet meals onboard, and wine tastings that celebrate the local flavors.

Community and Social Interaction:

The communal atmosphere onboard Rhine River cruises fosters social interaction. Passengers from around the world come together, creating a sense of community as they share experiences and create lasting connections.

Guided Excursions:

Shore excursions provide passengers with guided tours of historical sites, cultural landmarks, and natural wonders. Knowledgeable guides enhance the understanding of the destinations visited.

Comfort and Convenience:

River cruises offer a comfortable and convenient way to explore multiple destinations without the need for constant packing and unpacking. The ship becomes a floating hotel, providing a home base for travelers.

Flexibility and Choice:

Rhine River cruises come in various durations and itineraries, catering to different preferences. Whether seeking a short getaway or an extended exploration, passengers can choose the cruise that suits their schedule and interests.

Environmental Impact:

River cruises are often considered more environmentally friendly than some other forms of travel. The ships are designed with sustainability in mind, and the focus on river navigation minimizes the ecological impact.

Chapter One
PLANNING YOUR RHINE ADVENTURE

CHOOSING THE RIGHT CRUISE PACKAGE

Define Your Priorities:

Start by identifying your travel priorities. Are you seeking historical immersion, culinary delights, or scenic landscapes? Understanding your preferences will guide you towards a cruise package that caters to your specific interests.

Duration and Itinerary:

Rhine River cruises vary in duration and itineraries. Consider how much time you have available and the destinations you wish to explore. Some cruises focus on specific regions, while others cover a broader stretch of the Rhine. Choose a package that aligns with your desired travel duration and the places you want to visit.

Cruise Style:

Rhine River cruises come in different styles, ranging from luxury cruises with gourmet dining to more casual and family-friendly options. Research the onboard amenities, dining options, and entertainment to find a cruise style that matches your preferences and budget.

Shore Excursions:

Evaluate the included shore excursions. These guided tours offer opportunities to explore historical sites, charming towns, and scenic spots along the Rhine. Consider the variety and depth of excursions offered in each package to ensure they align with your interests.

Cabin Types:

Cruise packages offer various cabin types, from standard rooms to suites with panoramic views. Consider the level of comfort you desire and whether you prefer a private balcony for uninterrupted scenic views.

Understand the cabin options available in each package to make an informed decision.

Onboard Activities:

Explore the onboard activities and entertainment options. Some cruises feature lectures, cooking classes, or live performances, enhancing the cultural experience.

Choose a package with activities that resonate with your interests, ensuring a well-rounded and enjoyable journey.

Dining Options:

Culinary experiences are a highlight of Rhine River cruises. Research the dining options offered in each package, from gourmet restaurants to casual eateries. Consider any special dietary requirements and choose a cruise with dining choices that suit your preferences.

Cruise Company Reputation:

Research the reputation of cruise companies offering Rhine River packages. Reviews and testimonials from fellow travelers can provide valuable insights into the quality of service, onboard experience, and the overall satisfaction of past passengers.

Inclusions and Exclusions:

Scrutinize the inclusions and exclusions of each cruise package. Some may include gratuities, Wi-Fi, or beverages, while others might require additional payments for these amenities.

Understanding the overall cost and what is covered in the package ensures transparency and avoids surprises.

Flexible Booking Policies:

In uncertain times, having flexible booking policies is essential. Check the cancellation and refund policies of each cruise package to ensure you have the flexibility to adapt your plans if needed.

BEST TIME TO VISIT THE RHINE RIVER

The Rhine River, with its picturesque landscapes, historic castles, and charming vineyards, is a timeless destination. To ensure you experience the full splendor of this iconic river, it's essential to choose the best time to embark on your Rhine adventure.

Spring Awakening (April to June):

Spring is a magical time along the Rhine. As nature awakens, the vineyards burst into vibrant shades of green, and blossoms adorn the riverbanks.

The weather is mild, and temperatures gradually rise, making it an ideal season for exploring charming towns and enjoying outdoor activities. Cruising the Rhine during spring offers a tapestry of colors and a sense of renewal.

Summer Bliss (July to August):

Summer is the high season for Rhine River cruises, and for good reason. The days are long, temperatures are warm, and the riverbanks are alive with activity.

Cruise under the clear blue skies, savoring the beauty of the landscape in its full glory. Be prepared for more fellow travelers, especially in popular ports, as this is when the Rhine shines brightest.

Autumn Splendor (September to October):

Autumn transforms the Rhine into a canvas of warm hues. The vineyards turn shades of red and gold, and the air carries a crispness that adds to the enchantment.

The crowds thin out compared to summer, providing a more relaxed experience. Fall is also harvest time in the vineyards, offering a chance to indulge in the region's celebrated wines.

Winter Magic (November to March):

Winter along the Rhine has its own charm. The riverbanks may be dusted with snow, creating a serene and cozy atmosphere.

While some cruise lines may have reduced schedules during winter, those venturing during this time can enjoy the festive holiday markets that adorn towns along the Rhine. Experience the magic of Christmas markets and the Rhine's serene winter beauty.

Considerations for Each Season:

Spring: Ideal for nature lovers and those seeking a vibrant landscape.

Summer: Perfect for long days of exploration and enjoying the liveliness of the river.

Autumn: A photographer's delight with stunning fall foliage and fewer crowds.

Winter: Offers a unique and festive atmosphere with Christmas markets.

Weather and River Conditions:

Keep in mind that weather conditions and water levels can impact your Rhine River experience. While summer ensures the most reliable conditions, occasional rain may lead to higher water levels. Spring and autumn may offer more varied weather, so packing layers is advisable.

Cruise Events and Festivals:

Consider any special events or festivals along the Rhine during your preferred time. This may influence your decision, especially if you're interested in experiencing local traditions and celebrations.

DURATION OF THE CRUISE

A Rhine River cruise is a captivating odyssey through history, culture, and breathtaking landscapes. The duration of your cruise plays a pivotal role in shaping your experience, offering different facets of this iconic river. Here's a guide to help you determine the ideal duration for your Rhine adventure.

Short and Sweet Getaways (3 to 5 Days):

Short-duration cruises are perfect for those with limited time but a fervent desire to experience the essence of the Rhine.

These cruises typically focus on a specific section of the river, often between iconic cities like Amsterdam and Cologne. Ideal for a quick escape, you'll get a taste of the Rhine's charm without an extensive time commitment.

Week-Long Escapades (7 Days):

Opting for a week-long Rhine River cruise opens up a more comprehensive exploration. Covering significant stretches of the river, these cruises often include visits to multiple countries and renowned cities such as Strasbourg, Basel, and Koblenz. A seven-day cruise allows for a deeper immersion into the cultural tapestry of the Rhine's riverbanks.

Extended Journeys (10 Days or More):

For a more leisurely pace and a thorough exploration of the Rhine's treasures, consider an extended cruise lasting 10 days or more. This duration provides ample time for in-depth excursions, allowing you to delve into the rich history, architecture, and landscapes along the entire course of the Rhine.

Extended cruises often reach the river's source in the Swiss Alps, offering a truly comprehensive experience.

Considerations for Each Duration:

Short Cruises: Ideal for a quick getaway or those new to river cruising.

Week-Long Cruises: Balances exploration and relaxation, covering significant portions of the Rhine.

Extended Journeys: Perfect for enthusiasts seeking a comprehensive Rhine experience with more time for immersive excursions.

Themes and Special Cruises:

Some cruise lines offer themed or special interest cruises that may extend beyond the typical durations. These can include wine cruises, holiday-themed voyages, or cruises focused on cultural events. Consider if any specific theme aligns with your interests.

Budget and Time Constraints:

Your budget and available time play crucial roles in choosing the duration. Shorter cruises may be more budget-friendly and convenient for those with limited vacation time.

VISA AND DOCUMENTATION

Understanding Schengen Visa Requirements:

If your Rhine River cruise includes multiple Schengen countries, ensure you are aware of the Schengen Visa requirements.

Many river cruises stop in cities spanning different countries, and a Schengen Visa allows you to move freely within these designated areas.

Check Cruise Itinerary and Ports:

Thoroughly review your cruise itinerary, as it will outline the ports of call and countries you'll visit. Each country may have different visa requirements, so understanding the complete journey is crucial. Common ports along the Rhine include Amsterdam, Cologne, Strasbourg, Basel, and more.

Schengen Area Countries along the Rhine:

Major cities along the Rhine are often located in Schengen countries like Germany, Netherlands, France, and Switzerland. If your cruise extends to non-Schengen areas, such as parts of Switzerland, be aware of specific entry requirements.

Schengen Visa Application Process:

Initiate the Schengen Visa application process well in advance. This typically involves providing proof of travel arrangements, accommodation reservations, travel insurance, financial means, and a detailed itinerary. Consult the respective consulate or embassy for accurate and up-to-date information.

Non-Schengen Countries:

If your cruise extends to non-Schengen countries, research and comply with the visa regulations of those specific nations. Switzerland, for example, is not part of the EU but is a popular destination along the Rhine.

Travel Insurance and Health Documentation:

Ensure you have comprehensive travel insurance that covers medical emergencies. Some countries may also require proof of specific vaccinations or health documentation; check these requirements well in advance.

Passport Validity:

Check the validity of your passport. Many countries require at least six months of validity beyond your planned departure date. Renew your passport if needed, ensuring it aligns with the travel duration.

Consult with Cruise Operator:

Reach out to your cruise operator for guidance. They often have experienced staff who can provide insights into visa requirements and may assist with the application process.

Plan Well in Advance:

Visa processing times vary, and it's advisable to start the application process well in advance of your intended travel date. This helps avoid last-minute complications and ensures a stress-free journey.

Navigating visa and documentation requirements for a Rhine River cruise may seem intricate, but thorough preparation ensures you can fully savor the wonders of this iconic waterway. With the right paperwork in place, your Rhine adventure will be a seamless and memorable experience.

BOOKING TIPS AND DISCOUNTS

Booking a Rhine River cruise is more than reserving a cabin; it's about curating an immersive experience along one of Europe's most enchanting waterways. This guide unveils essential booking tips and strategies to ensure your Rhine adventure exceeds expectations.

Book Early for Preferred Cabins:

Rhine River cruises are immensely popular, especially during peak seasons. Secure your preferred cabin by booking well in advance.

This not only ensures prime accommodation but may also unlock early booking discounts.

Flexible Dates for Optimal Savings:

Flexibility with travel dates can significantly impact your cruise cost. Consider sailing during the shoulder seasons or off-peak times to capitalize on lower prices. Some cruise lines offer discounts for midweek departures or less popular months.

Leverage Off-Season Bargains:

While summer is peak cruise season, exploring the Rhine in the off-season can be equally enchanting. Winter cruises present a different charm with festive markets along the riverbanks. Take advantage of off-season discounts and fewer crowds.

Monitor Cruise Line Promotions:

Stay vigilant for promotions offered by cruise lines. These may include early booking incentives, onboard credits, or discounted airfare. Subscribe to newsletters and follow cruise operators on social media to catch exclusive deals.

Consider Group Discounts:

Traveling with a group of friends or family? Inquire about group discounts. Some cruise lines provide reduced rates, complimentary amenities, or exclusive group events for parties booking multiple cabins.

Last-Minute Deals for Spontaneous Travelers:

If your schedule allows for spontaneity, explore last-minute deals. Cruise lines may offer significant discounts to fill remaining cabins closer to departure dates. However, this approach requires flexibility and may not guarantee specific cabin choices.

Bundle with Airfare and Excursions:

Some cruise packages include airfare and shore excursions. Bundling these components can result in cost savings compared to booking them separately. Evaluate the overall package to determine its value.

Take Advantage of Cruise Loyalty Programs:

If you're a frequent cruiser or considering future voyages, explore cruise loyalty programs.

Accumulating points with a specific cruise line can lead to perks such as cabin upgrades, onboard credits, and even exclusive access to events.

Consult with Travel Agents:

Travel agents often have access to exclusive deals and insights. Their expertise can help you navigate various cruise options, understand promotions, and secure additional amenities.

Review Refund and Cancellation Policies:

Before finalizing your booking, carefully review the refund and cancellation policies. Understand the terms in case unexpected circumstances require itinerary adjustments.

Unlocking the best booking tips and discounts for your Rhine River cruise ensures you not only secure an inviting cabin but also embark on a journey infused with value and savings. By strategically navigating the booking process, your Rhine adventure becomes a seamless and rewarding experience.

Chapter Two
RHINE RIVER ESSENTIALS
GEOGRAPHY AND TOPOGRAPHY

A River's Tale:

The Rhine River, often referred to as the "Father Rhine," meanders through the heart of Europe, spanning over 800 miles. Originating in the Swiss Alps, its course takes it through six countries: Switzerland, Liechtenstein, Austria, Germany, France, and the Netherlands.

Swiss Splendor:

The Rhine's journey begins in the southeastern Swiss Alps, where the two main tributaries, the Vorderrhein and Hinterrhein, converge at the Alpine Lake Tomasee. The pristine Swiss landscapes form a picturesque prologue to the river's narrative.

The Enchanting Middle Rhine:

As the Rhine flows into Germany, it transforms into the Middle Rhine, a UNESCO World Heritage site renowned for its castles, vineyards, and romantic landscapes. The Lorelei Rock, a legendary steep slate rock, adds a touch of mystique to this segment.

Vineyard-Carpeted Hills:

The Rhine Gorge, often hailed as the "Romantic Rhine," showcases steep vineyard-covered hills that produce some of the finest wines. The terraced vineyards contribute to the region's postcard-perfect allure.

Architectural Symphony:

Germany's Rhineland is adorned with a captivating array of castles and fortresses perched on hills overlooking the river. Each castle tells a story of medieval power struggles, adding a historical dimension to the cruise.

Dutch Delta:

As the Rhine nears its end, it enters the Netherlands, where it transforms into a vast delta system. The river splits into several distributaries, forming a network of channels and islands known for their distinctive landscapes and vibrant cities.

Gateway to the Sea:

The Rhine Delta eventually empties into the North Sea, marking the culmination of its majestic journey. The vast estuarine region supports unique ecosystems and plays a crucial role in the region's maritime dynamics.

Navigating Locks and Weirs:

Throughout its course, the Rhine encounters a series of locks and weirs, essential for regulating water levels and facilitating navigation. These engineering marvels showcase the intricate infrastructure that supports the bustling river traffic.

Rhine's Contribution to Trade:

Historically, the Rhine served as a vital trade route, connecting inland regions with coastal ports. Its economic significance has endured, and today, the river facilitates the transportation of goods and fuels the economies of the countries it traverses.

Ecological Diversity:

The Rhine's diverse ecosystems, from alpine headwaters to estuarine habitats, harbor a rich array of flora and fauna. Conservation efforts have led to the restoration of biodiversity, making the river a haven for nature enthusiasts.

Understanding the geography and topography of the Rhine River adds depth to the anticipation of your cruise. As you navigate its varied landscapes, from Alpine sources to the Dutch delta, you embark on a journey that unfolds the geographical poetry etched into the Rhine's very essence.

NAVIGATING THE RHINE: PORTS AND ITINERARY OPTIONS

Amsterdam: The Gateway to Your Rhine Adventure

Canals and Cobblestones: A Prelude to Romance:

Amsterdam's iconic canals crisscross the city, creating a backdrop that is both romantic and timeless. Picture-perfect bridges, lined with historic buildings, invite leisurely strolls along cobblestone streets.

Cultural Treasures: From Rembrandt to Anne Frank:

Immerse yourself in Amsterdam's cultural wealth. The Rijksmuseum showcases Dutch masterpieces, while the Van Gogh Museum pays tribute to the iconic artist. Don't miss the poignant visit to the Anne Frank House, a testament to resilience.

Iconic Landmarks: Embracing the Old and the New:

Amsterdam seamlessly blends its historic charm with modern marvels. The Royal Palace at Dam Square stands as a testament to the city's regal past, while the futuristic architecture of the Eye Filmmuseum points towards Amsterdam's progressive spirit.

Jordaan: Bohemian Bliss on the Water:

The Jordaan district unveils Amsterdam's bohemian side. Quaint cafes, boutique shops, and art galleries line the narrow streets, offering an authentic local experience. Explore the Anne Frank House in this district, a poignant reminder of history.

Floating Flower Paradise: Bloemenmarkt:

Bloemenmarkt, the world's only floating flower market, bursts with a kaleidoscope of colors. Tulips, the symbol of the Netherlands, steal the show. Immerse yourself in the fragrant beauty of the flower stalls.

Canal Cruises: Navigating Amsterdam's Waterways:

A visit to Amsterdam is incomplete without a canal cruise. Drift along the serene waters, passing under charming bridges and past historic landmarks. It's a unique perspective that unveils the city's beauty from a different angle.

Vibrant Nightlife: From Pubs to Red-Light District:

As the sun sets, Amsterdam's vibrant nightlife comes to life. Enjoy a leisurely drink in one of the city's cozy pubs or explore the eclectic Red-Light District, known for its distinctive energy and entertainment.

Culinary Delights: Dutch Treats and International Cuisine:

Amsterdam's culinary scene is a delightful fusion of traditional Dutch treats and global gastronomy. Sample stroopwafels at local markets, indulge in Dutch cheeses, and savor diverse international cuisines.

Strasbourg: A Blend of French and German Flair

Nestled along the banks of the Rhine River, Strasbourg stands as a testament to the fascinating confluence of French and German cultures.

Let's uncover the unique charm of Strasbourg, a city that seamlessly marries the elegance of France with the warmth of German hospitality.

Historical Tapestry: Strasbourg Cathedral:

Dominating the skyline, Strasbourg Cathedral is a Gothic masterpiece that has witnessed centuries of history.

Its intricate façade and soaring spire are symbolic of the city's resilience and architectural prowess.

La Petite France: A Fairytale District:

Stroll through the enchanting district of La Petite France, where half-timbered houses, flower-draped windows, and winding canals transport you to a fairytale setting.

Quaint cafes and artisan shops beckon, inviting you to savor the charm of this picturesque neighborhood.

European Quarter: A Symbol of Unity:

Strasbourg serves as a symbolic seat of European unity, hosting key institutions like the European Parliament. The European Quarter reflects a commitment to collaboration and diplomacy, showcasing modern architecture and fostering a sense of shared purpose.

The Alsatian Museum: A Cultural Journey:

Immerse yourself in the rich tapestry of Alsatian heritage at The Alsatian Museum. From traditional costumes to artisanal crafts, the museum offers a captivating journey through the region's cultural evolution.

Culinary Delights: A Fusion of Tastes:

Strasbourg's gastronomy is a delightful fusion of French and German influences. Indulge in Alsatian specialties like flammekueche (a type of tart) and choucroute garnie (sauerkraut with sausages), accompanied by the region's renowned wines.

River Ill: A Tranquil Waterway:

The River Ill meanders through Strasbourg, providing a serene backdrop to the city's beauty. Enjoy a leisurely boat cruise along the river, passing under charming bridges and admiring the reflections of historic buildings.

Strasbourg's Christmas Markets: A Winter Wonderland:

Experience the magic of Strasbourg during the festive season. The city's Christmas markets, among the oldest in Europe, transform Strasbourg into a winter wonderland. Twinkling lights, festive stalls, and the scent of mulled wine create an enchanting atmosphere.

Bilingual Atmosphere: A Cultural Crossroads:

Strasbourg's bilingual ambiance reflects its unique position as a cultural crossroads. French and German coexist seamlessly, creating a welcoming environment where both languages are spoken and celebrated.

The Romantic Rhine: Castles, Vineyards, and Fairytale Villages

Lorelei Rock: A Siren's Song:

Stand in awe of the Lorelei Rock, a mystical cliff overlooking the Rhine. Legend has it that a siren named Lorelei sang bewitching melodies, luring sailors to their fate. Today, this iconic site offers breathtaking views of the river's meandering course.

Rhine Castles: Sentinels of the Past:

The Rhine is adorned with medieval castles perched atop vine-covered hills. Explore iconic fortresses like Marksburg and Burg Rheinstein, each with its own saga of knights, battles, and romantic legends. Marvel at their towers and turrets that stand as silent witnesses to centuries gone by.

Vineyards in Rüdesheim: A Wine Lover's Paradise:

Rüdesheim is a gateway to the captivating world of Rhine wines. Wander through terraced vineyards, where Riesling grapes flourish. Visit renowned wineries to indulge in tastings, savoring the flavors of wines cultivated on the fertile slopes of the Rhine Valley.

Fairytale Villages: A Step Back in Time:

Cruise past fairytale villages like Bacharach and St. Goar, where half-timbered houses and cobblestone streets transport you to an era of knights and maidens. Experience the charm of these well-preserved hamlets that epitomize the Romantic Rhine's idyllic allure.

Boppard's Rhine Promenade: A Riverside Retreat:

Boppard welcomes you with its Rhine Promenade, a scenic stretch along the riverbank. Admire the panoramic views, stroll through charming gardens, and feel the gentle breeze as you immerse yourself in the tranquility of this riverside retreat.

Cruise Experiences: Navigating History:

Embark on a river cruise that winds through the heart of the Romantic Rhine. Sail past the iconic Lorelei Rock, witness the majesty of castles, and savor the changing landscapes that tell stories of battles, romance, and the enduring spirit of the region.

Koblenz: Confluence of Cultures:

Explore Koblenz, where the Rhine and Moselle rivers converge. Discover historic squares, wander through the Old Town, and ascend to the Ehrenbreitstein Fortress for panoramic vistas. Koblenz symbolizes the confluence of cultures and the rich tapestry of Rhine history.

Rhine in Flames: A Spectacular Celebration:

Immerse yourself in the dazzling spectacle of Rhine in Flames, an annual event where the river is illuminated by fireworks, casting a magical glow on the castles, vineyards, and villages. It's a celebration of the Romantic Rhine's enduring allure.

The Romantic Rhine beckons with its tales of love, valor, and timeless beauty. Whether you're drawn to the legends of castles, the flavors of local wines, or the charm of fairytale villages, this stretch of the Rhine invites you to embark on a journey that transcends time and captures the essence of romance.

Cologne: A Tale of Cathedrals and Culture

Cologne Cathedral: Gothic Majesty:

Behold the awe-inspiring Cologne Cathedral, a Gothic masterpiece that dominates the skyline. Delve into the history of this UNESCO World Heritage site, from its construction in the 13th century to the intricate details of its façade.

Explore the cathedral's interior, home to stunning stained glass windows and the Shrine of the Three Kings.

Old Town (Altstadt): Timeless Charm:

Wander through the narrow streets of Cologne's Old Town, where medieval architecture meets modern flair. Discover colorful houses, bustling squares, and hidden gems like the historic Fish Market.

Immerse yourself in the lively atmosphere of this district that effortlessly marries tradition with a contemporary vibe.

Rhine Promenade: A Riverside Stroll:

Experience the Rhine Promenade, a scenic riverfront pathway offering panoramic views of the water and the cityscape. Join locals and visitors alike in leisurely strolls, enjoy outdoor cafes, and feel the pulse of the city while soaking in the tranquility of the river.

Museum Ludwig: Artistic Brilliance:

Indulge your artistic senses at the Museum Ludwig, a cultural gem housing an extensive collection of modern and contemporary art.

From Picasso to Warhol, the museum showcases diverse masterpieces that reflect the evolution of artistic expression over the years.

Cologne's Culinary Delights: Gastronomic Pleasures:

Delight your taste buds with Cologne's culinary offerings. Sample traditional Kölsch beer in one of the local breweries, savor regional specialties like Himmel un Ääd (Heaven and Earth), and explore the city's vibrant food scene that caters to every palate.

Lively Markets: Shopping Extravaganza:

Dive into Cologne's markets, each with its unique character. From the bustling Cologne Cathedral Christmas Market to the eclectic offerings at the Belgian Quarter's flea market, experience the city's lively markets that reflect its dynamic and diverse spirit.

Cologne's Festivals and Events: Celebrating Diversity:

Discover Cologne's festive side with a calendar filled with events celebrating diversity. From the Cologne Carnival, one of the largest street festivals in Europe, to the lit-up nights during the Cologne Lights, the city knows how to celebrate and invite everyone to join the party.

Local Vibes: Cologne's Neighborhoods:

Explore the distinct neighborhoods that make up Cologne's dynamic mosaic. From the trendy Ehrenfeld to the multicultural Agnesviertel, each area contributes to the city's rich tapestry of culture, arts, and lifestyles.

Basel: Where the Rhine Journey Concludes

Basel's Old Town: A Stroll Through History:

Step into Basel's Old Town, a charming district where medieval history blends seamlessly with contemporary life. Explore narrow cobblestone streets, discover medieval buildings like the Basel Minster, and experience the timeless allure of this historic quarter.

Rhine River Cruises: Basel's Nautical Hub:

Delve into Basel's role as a nautical hub on the Rhine. Learn about the city's significance as a starting or ending point for Rhine River cruises, with its well-equipped ports and picturesque riverfront providing a fitting backdrop to the conclusion of your journey.

Art and Culture: Basel's Museums and Galleries:

Immerse yourself in Basel's vibrant cultural scene, home to world-renowned museums like the Kunstmuseum and Fondation Beyeler.

Discover an extensive collection of art spanning centuries, from classical masterpieces to contemporary works, making Basel a haven for art enthusiasts.

Rhine Bridges: Connecting Cultures:

Marvel at Basel's iconic Rhine bridges that span the river, serving as symbolic connections between different cultures and neighborhoods. Learn about the history of these bridges and their role in shaping the city's identity.

Swiss Cuisine: Gastronomic Delights:

Indulge your taste buds with Basel's culinary offerings. Experience Swiss gastronomy at local restaurants, savoring dishes like fondue and raclette. Dive into the vibrant food scene that mirrors Basel's cultural diversity.

Marktplatz and Rathaus: Civic Elegance:

Visit the Marktplatz, Basel's central square, surrounded by architectural gems like the Rathaus (Town Hall). Explore the vibrant market, witness local life unfolding, and absorb the civic elegance that defines this historical square.

Rhine Park: Scenic Serenity:

Unwind in Basel's Rhine Park, a picturesque green space along the riverbanks. Enjoy a leisurely stroll, soak in the breathtaking views of the Rhine, and reflect on the experiences of your river cruise against the backdrop of this serene setting.

Cultural Events and Festivals: Basel's Celebratory Spirit:

Discover Basel's festive side with a peek into its calendar of cultural events and festivals. From the renowned Art Basel fair to the vibrant Fasnacht carnival, experience the city's dynamic and celebratory spirit.

PACKING TIPS AND ESSENTIALS

Weather-Appropriate Attire:

Understand the climate along the Rhine and pack accordingly. Layers are key as temperatures can vary. Bring comfortable walking shoes for shore excursions and formal attire for onboard events.

Power Adapters and Chargers:

Ensure you have the right power adapters for the countries you'll visit. Pack chargers for your devices and consider a portable charger for day trips.

Travel Documents:

Keep all necessary travel documents in one secure place. This includes your passport, cruise tickets, travel insurance, and any required visas.

Medications and First Aid Kit:

Bring any prescription medications you need and a basic first aid kit. Include items like pain relievers, seasickness medication, and bandages.

Daypack or Tote Bag:

A small daypack or tote bag is handy for excursions. Pack essentials like a water bottle, sunscreen, a hat, and your camera to capture the picturesque moments along the Rhine.

Travel-Sized Toiletries:

Opt for travel-sized toiletries to save space. Include essentials like toothpaste, shampoo, and sunscreen. Most cruises provide basic toiletries, but having your preferred products can add a personal touch.

Appropriate Electronics:

Pack essential electronics such as your camera, smartphone, and perhaps a tablet or e-reader for downtime. Consider noise-canceling headphones for a peaceful cruise experience.

Swimwear and Leisure Wear:

If your cruise includes amenities like a pool or spa, pack swimwear. Leisure wear for relaxing onboard or exploring port cities adds comfort to your cruise wardrobe.

Reusable Water Bottle:

Stay hydrated during your excursions by bringing a reusable water bottle. Some cruise lines may provide water, but having your bottle ensures you stay refreshed throughout the day.

Travel Guide and Maps:

Carry a travel guide or download relevant apps to enhance your understanding of the regions you'll visit. Maps can be helpful for self-guided exploration in port cities.

Snacks and Refreshments:

Pack some snacks for the times between meals or when exploring onshore. Consider local treats from the regions you'll visit for a delightful culinary experience.

Travel Insurance Details

Have a copy of your travel insurance details easily accessible. This includes contact information and policy numbers for any unforeseen circumstances.

Binoculars:

Enjoy scenic views along the Rhine with a pair of binoculars. Spot castles, vineyards, and other landmarks from the comfort of your cruise ship.

Reading Material or Journal:

Bring a good book or journal to unwind during leisure moments. Whether you prefer literary escapes or documenting your travel experiences, having reading material adds a personal touch.

Luggage Tags and Identification:

Attach clear and durable luggage tags to your bags. Ensure your identification is easily visible, and consider labeling your belongings to avoid mix-ups.

As you prepare for your Rhine River cruise, these packing tips and essentials will help you make the most of your journey. From practical necessities to personal comforts, thoughtful packing ensures you're ready to embrace the enchanting experience that awaits along the scenic Rhine

Chapter Three
EMBARKING ON THE RHINE JOURNEY

DEPARTURE PORTS AND EMBARKATION PROCEDURES

Amsterdam: The Gateway to Rhine Magic:

Amsterdam, with its iconic canals and vibrant atmosphere, often serves as a primary departure port for Rhine River cruises.

Begin your journey amid the picturesque Dutch scenery, exploring the city's rich history and cultural gems before setting sail.

Basel: The Swiss Starting Point:

Basel, nestled on the banks of the Rhine in Switzerland, is another common departure port. Discover the city's unique blend of Swiss and German influences, from medieval old town charm to modern cultural attractions, before embarking on your cruise.

Cologne: Start Amidst Gothic Splendor:

Embark on your Rhine adventure from Cologne, where the imposing Cologne Cathedral provides a stunning backdrop. Explore this German city's historical landmarks, including the cathedral itself, before boarding your cruise.

Strasbourg: French Flair along the Rhine:

Strasbourg, with its blend of French and German influences, offers a departure point rich in cultural diversity. Delight in the charm of Alsatian architecture and the unique atmosphere of this city before commencing your Rhine River exploration.

Rhine Gorge Departures:

Some cruises embark from picturesque locations within the Rhine Gorge itself. Imagine starting your journey surrounded by the dramatic landscapes, vineyard-covered hills, and medieval castles that characterize this enchanting stretch of the Rhine.

Navigating Embarkation Procedures

Embarkation day sets the tone for your Rhine River cruise, and understanding the procedures ensures a seamless start to your adventure:

Check-In and Documentation:

Arrive at the departure port with ample time for check-in. Have your cruise documents, identification, and any necessary visas or travel permits ready for efficient processing.

Luggage Drop-Off:

Most cruises offer luggage drop-off services, allowing you to part ways with your bags upon arrival. Ensure your luggage is properly tagged with your cabin details for hassle-free delivery to your room.

Security and Boarding:

Navigate security procedures with ease, adhering to guidelines similar to those at airports. Once through security, proceed to the boarding area where you'll be welcomed by the ship's staff.

Welcome Aboard:

Experience the warm hospitality of the cruise staff as you step onto the ship. Enjoy a welcome drink, receive your room key, and begin immersing yourself in the cruise atmosphere.

Safety Briefing:

Attend the mandatory safety briefing to familiarize yourself with emergency procedures. Cruise staff will guide you through safety measures, ensuring a secure and enjoyable journey.

Settling into Your Cabin:

Once onboard, take a moment to settle into your cabin. Unpack, explore the amenities, and begin embracing the comfort of your floating home for the duration of the cruise.

Embarking on a Rhine River cruise is a seamless process when armed with knowledge about departure ports and embarkation procedures. As you step aboard your chosen cruise ship, the anticipation of the adventures that lie ahead sets the stage for an extraordinary journey along the captivating Rhine.

THE RIVER CRUISE SHIP EXPERIENCE

Intimate Elegance Afloat:

River cruise ships, designed for intimacy and elegance, redefine the cruising experience. With smaller passenger capacities compared to ocean liners, these vessels create an atmosphere of camaraderie and exclusivity, ensuring personalized attention for each guest.

Staterooms with a View:

Unwind in staterooms designed for both comfort and scenic appreciation. Picture expansive windows or private balconies that offer uninterrupted views of the picturesque Rhine landscapes, allowing you to wake up to breathtaking river panoramas every day.

Gourmet Dining on the Rhine:

Culinary excellence is a cornerstone of the river cruise experience. Indulge in gourmet dining featuring locally inspired dishes, often crafted with fresh, regional ingredients. Savor exquisite flavors in elegant dining rooms while floating along the serene Rhine.

Relaxation Spaces:

Cruise ships along the Rhine provide an array of relaxation spaces. From sun decks with panoramic views to cozy lounges, find your perfect spot to unwind. Enjoy a book, sip a drink, or simply soak in the ambiance as the picturesque riverside scenery glides by.

Cultural Enrichment Onboard:

Immerse yourself in the rich cultural tapestry of the Rhine right on the ship. Many cruises offer onboard lectures, performances, and demonstrations, providing insights into the history, art, and traditions of the regions you'll explore.

Wellness and Leisure:

Stay rejuvenated with onboard wellness facilities. From fitness centers with river views to relaxing spas, river cruise ships prioritize your well-being. Take a dip in the pool or indulge in a soothing massage as you cruise along the tranquil Rhine waters.

Excursion Planning and Expert Guides:

Dedicated staff and expert guides assist in planning onshore excursions, ensuring you make the most of your time at each port of call.

These knowledgeable guides provide insights into the local culture, history, and attractions, enhancing your overall experience.

Nightly Entertainment:

Evenings aboard a Rhine River cruise come alive with entertainment. Enjoy live music, themed events, and performances that add a touch of glamour to your nights on the water. Whether it's a musical recital or a themed costume party, the cruise ship becomes a stage for memorable experiences.

All-Inclusive Luxury:

Many river cruises operate on an all-inclusive model, covering meals, beverages, shore excursions, and gratuities. This ensures a hassle-free experience, allowing you to focus on enjoying the journey without worrying about additional costs.

Connecting with Fellow Travelers:

River cruises foster a sense of community. Share experiences and make new friends with like-minded travelers during communal meals, onboard activities, and shore excursions. The intimate setting encourages connections that often extend beyond the duration of the cruise.

YOUR STATEROOM: A HOME ON THE WATER

Elegance Meets Functionality:

Your stateroom is a harmonious blend of elegance and functionality. Discover thoughtfully designed spaces where aesthetics meet practicality. From tasteful furnishings to clever storage solutions, every detail is curated for your comfort.

Scenic Views from Every Angle:

Open the curtains to reveal panoramic views of the Rhine's picturesque landscapes. Many staterooms feature large windows or private balconies, allowing you to immerse yourself in the ever-changing scenery as the ship gracefully glides along the river.

Categories of Staterooms:

Rhine River cruises offer a variety of stateroom categories to suit different preferences and budgets. From cozy interior cabins ideal for those seeking a peaceful retreat to lavish suites with expansive balconies, choose the accommodation that aligns with your vision of a perfect cruise.

A Personal Oasis:

Your stateroom is more than just a place to sleep; it's a personal oasis. Sink into plush bedding, unwind in comfortable seating areas, and relish the privacy of your own space. The soothing ambiance creates a sanctuary where you can rejuvenate after each day's adventures.

Modern Amenities:

Enjoy modern amenities at your fingertips. High-quality linens, flat-screen TVs, and well-appointed bathrooms with rejuvenating toiletries elevate your stateroom experience. Indulge in the luxury of a floating hotel room that caters to your every need.

Tailored Services:

Staterooms on Rhine River cruises come with dedicated service. From attentive housekeeping to personalized touches, the crew ensures your space is always welcoming. Experience the warmth of hospitality as you return to a neatly prepared haven each day.

Private Balconies:

Opt for a stateroom with a private balcony to take your Rhine River experience to the next level. Step outside to breathe in the fresh river air, enjoy a morning coffee with sunrise views, or unwind with a glass of wine as the sun sets over the tranquil waters.

Suite Life:

For those seeking the epitome of luxury, suites on Rhine River cruises redefine opulence. Spacious layouts, enhanced amenities, and attentive service create a haven of indulgence. Experience the suite life with exclusive privileges and breathtaking views.

In-Room Dining:

Revel in the convenience of in-room dining. Whether it's a leisurely breakfast on your balcony or a cozy dinner after a day of exploration, the option to enjoy delectable meals in the privacy of your stateroom adds an extra layer of comfort to your cruise.

Sleeping Under the Stars:

Some staterooms offer innovative features like retractable ceilings or skylights, allowing you to sleep under the stars. Immerse yourself in the celestial beauty of the night sky while nestled in the comfort of your bed, creating an enchanting and romantic atmosphere.

Your stateroom is more than accommodation; it's your private retreat on the Rhine. As you embark on this river cruise adventure, relish the joy of returning to a beautifully appointed space that complements the breathtaking landscapes outside. Each stateroom is a haven—a home on the water, inviting you to create lasting memories along the enchanting banks of the Rhine.

Chapter Four
RHINE RIVER REGIONS AND DESTINATIONS

UPPER RHINE: BASEL TO STRASBOURG

Embark on an enchanting journey through the Upper Rhine, where the river meanders gracefully between the charming cities of Basel and Strasbourg. we delve into the allure of this stretch, uncovering the cultural richness, historical wonders, and scenic delights that await every traveler along the banks of the majestic Rhine.

Basel: Gateway to Rhineland Adventure

Switzerland's Cultural Hub:

Basel serves as the cultural gateway to the Rhine adventure. Explore its vibrant art scene, with world-class museums like Kunstmuseum and Fondation Beyeler, or stroll through the medieval Old Town, where history whispers through cobblestone streets.

Cruising the Rhine from Basel

Setting Sail:

Your journey commences in Basel, where the ship gracefully sets sail on the Rhine's glistening waters. As you cruise upstream, be captivated by the scenic beauty of vineyard-covered hills, picturesque villages, and the promise of discoveries around every bend.

Rhine's Vineyard-Covered Hills:

Witness the mesmerizing vineyard-covered hills that flank the Rhine. The Upper Rhine region is renowned for its wine production, and the landscape is a patchwork of lush greenery.

Immerse yourself in the beauty of terraced vineyards that produce some of the finest wines in the world.

Breisach: German Gem on the Rhine

Situated on the Rhine's eastern bank, Breisach invites you to step into a world of medieval charm. Explore the iconic St. Stephen's Cathedral, perched atop a hill, offering panoramic views of the surrounding vineyards and the Rhine Valley.

Colmar: The Little Venice of Alsace

Quaint Waterways:

Sail to Colmar, often referred to as the "Little Venice of Alsace." Marvel at its well-preserved medieval architecture and meander along cobblestone streets lined with half-timbered houses. The canals, reminiscent of Venice, add a touch of romance to this Alsatian gem.

Strasbourg: Where French and German Influences Converge

European Union Capital:

The journey culminates in Strasbourg, a city where French and German influences converge seamlessly. Strasbourg, the capital of the European Union, boasts a UNESCO-listed Old Town, dominated by the iconic Strasbourg Cathedral and charming timber-framed houses.

Exploring Strasbourg's Old Town

Historical Marvels:

Wander through Strasbourg's Old Town, known for its enchanting squares, such as Place Kléber and Place Gutenberg. Admire the intricate architecture of La Petite France, a quarter famous for its medieval half-timbered houses, canals, and flower-lined streets.

The Cathedral of Notre-Dame de Strasbourg

Architectural Splendor:

No visit to Strasbourg is complete without marveling at the Cathedral of Notre-Dame. Ascend to its observation platform for panoramic views of the city and the Rhine. The cathedral's intricate facade and stunning stained glass windows tell tales of centuries gone by.

Culinary Delights in Strasbourg

Gastronomic Pleasures:

Indulge in Alsatian culinary delights in Strasbourg. From traditional dishes like choucroute garnie to mouthwatering pastries, the city's gastronomy is a delightful blend of French and German influences. Quaint cafes and Michelin-starred restaurants await, promising a culinary journey to remember.

The Rhine's Endless Charms

A Tapestry Unfolding:

As your cruise through the Upper Rhine draws to a close in Strasbourg, reflect on the tapestry of experiences that have unfolded along this captivating stretch. From cultural riches to natural beauty, the Upper Rhine leaves an indelible mark on every traveler's heart.

MIDDLE RHINE: KOBLENZ TO MAINZ

Embark on an extraordinary journey through the heart of the Rhine as you navigate the Middle Rhine, a stretch renowned for its dramatic landscapes, medieval castles, and enchanting vineyards.

Koblenz: The Confluence City

Meeting of Waters:

Begin your adventure in Koblenz, where the Rhine and Moselle rivers converge. Explore the iconic Deutsches Eck, witness the Ehrenbreitstein Fortress towering over the river, and absorb the lively atmosphere of this historic confluence city.

Cruising the Romantic Middle Rhine

Scenic Splendors:

Setting sail from Koblenz, immerse yourself in the romantic allure of the Middle Rhine. Marvel at the majestic Lorelei Rock, a legendary siren's perch, and cruise through the UNESCO-listed Rhine Gorge, where vineyard-covered slopes and medieval castles create a fairy-tale landscape.

Rhine Gorge: A UNESCO World Heritage Site

Castle-Studded Hills:

Explore the Rhine Gorge, a UNESCO World Heritage Site, where the river winds its way through steep hills adorned with vineyards and crowned by the ruins of castles. Each castle has its own tale to tell, contributing to the region's rich tapestry of history.

Bacharach: A Medieval Gem

Half-Timbered Beauty:

Dock at Bacharach, a medieval gem nestled along the riverbanks. Stroll through its well-preserved half-timbered houses, visit Stahleck Castle, and absorb the charm of this town frozen in time.

Marksburg Castle: A Fortress Unyielding to Time

Timeless Grandeur:

Journey to Marksburg Castle, perched proudly above the Rhine. This perfectly preserved medieval fortress offers a glimpse into the Middle Ages, showcasing armor-clad knights' halls, strategic battlements, and breathtaking views of the river below.

Rüdesheim: Wine and Musical Magic

Vineyards and Song:

Dock in Rüdesheim, a town celebrated for its wine and musical heritage. Explore the vibrant Drosselgasse, a lively lane filled with wine taverns and live music.

Don't miss Siegfried's Mechanical Music Cabinet, a unique museum housing a remarkable collection of self-playing musical instruments.

Ehrenfels Castle and Assmannshausen

Riverbank Elegance:

Sail past the ruins of Ehrenfels Castle and the picturesque village of Assmannshausen. The Middle Rhine's captivating scenery unfolds as you navigate past terraced vineyards and charming riverside communities.

Gutenberg's Mainz: A Literary Legacy

Printing Revolution:

Conclude your journey in Mainz, a city with deep historical roots. Visit the Gutenberg Museum, dedicated to the inventor of the printing press, Johannes Gutenberg. Explore the city's Old Town, where medieval architecture and modern vitality harmoniously coexist.

Culinary Delights Along the Middle Rhine

Wine and Gastronomy:

Indulge in the culinary treasures of the Middle Rhine, renowned for its Riesling wines and regional specialties. From wine-tasting in vineyard terraces to savoring local delicacies in riverside cafes, the Middle Rhine offers a delectable journey for the palate.

Reflections on the Middle Rhine

A River of Legends:

As your Middle Rhine cruise draws to an end in Mainz, reflect on the legends, landscapes, and cultural richness that have unfolded along this mesmerizing stretch. The Middle Rhine invites you to immerse yourself in a tapestry of history, natural beauty, and timeless charm.

LOWER RHINE: DUSSELDORF TO AMSTERDAM

Embark on an unforgettable exploration of the Lower Rhine, a region brimming with cultural richness, picturesque landscapes, and vibrant cities, discover the enchanting journey from Düsseldorf to Amsterdam, where history, art, and scenic wonders converge.

Düsseldorf: Modern Elegance Along the Rhine

Artistic Flourish:

Begin your Lower Rhine adventure in Düsseldorf, a city that seamlessly blends modernity with tradition. Explore the renowned Königsallee, an upscale shopping boulevard, and immerse yourself in the city's vibrant art scene at the Kunstsammlung Nordrhein-Westfalen.

Krefeld: Silk and Textile Heritage

Textile Treasures:

Cruise to Krefeld, known for its historical silk and textile industry. Delve into the city's industrial past at the German Textile Museum, housed in a former silk mill. Explore the charming city center adorned with elegant villas and gardens.

Xanten: Roman Heritage on the Rhine

Archaeological Marvels:

Discover Xanten, a town with a rich Roman history. Visit the Archaeological Park, where reconstructed Roman buildings and artifacts transport you back in time. Explore the impressive Xanten Cathedral and stroll along the picturesque Rhine promenade.

Rees: A Riverside Gem

Riverside Tranquility:

Dock in Rees, a delightful town nestled along the riverbanks. Wander through its well-preserved medieval center, featuring timber-framed houses and the imposing Marienkirche. Enjoy a leisurely stroll along the Rhine promenade with panoramic river views.

Arnhem: A Bridge to History

Airborne Legacy:

Cruise to Arnhem, forever etched in history for the Battle of Arnhem during World War II. Explore the Airborne Museum and the iconic John Frost Bridge, witnessing the city's resilience and post-war revival.

Nijmegen: Oldest City in the Netherlands

Historical Charms:

Visit Nijmegen, the oldest city in the Netherlands. Explore the medieval Valkhof Park, home to remnants of a Roman temple and Charlemagne's chapel. Wander through the city center, adorned with historic buildings and lively squares.

Wageningen: Gardens and Serenity

Botanical Beauty:

Discover Wageningen, a town known for its botanical gardens and serene ambiance. Visit the Belmonte Arboretum, a haven of diverse plant species, and enjoy the tranquility of this picturesque Dutch town.

Utrecht: Canals, Cathedrals, and Culture

Canal Cruises:

Cruise to Utrecht, a city distinguished by its intricate canal system and rich cultural offerings. Explore the iconic Dom Tower, visit the Centraal Museum, and experience the charm of Utrecht's historic canals.

Amsterdam: Grand Finale Along the Waterways

Canal-Centric Capital:

Conclude your Lower Rhine journey in Amsterdam, the vibrant Dutch capital. Immerse yourself in the city's cultural treasures, from the Rijksmuseum to the Anne Frank House. Cruise along Amsterdam's iconic canals, discovering the unique architecture and lively atmosphere.

Culinary Delights Along the Lower Rhine

Diverse Gastronomy:

Indulge in the culinary offerings of the Lower Rhine, where a diverse range of flavors awaits. From Dutch cheeses to German delicacies, savor the regional gastronomy that adds a delightful dimension to your Rhine River cruise.

Reflections on the Lower Rhine

A Tapestry of Diversity:

Reflect on the diversity of experiences, from modern cityscapes to ancient Roman heritage, as your Lower Rhine cruise culminates in Amsterdam. The Lower Rhine invites you to explore its varied landscapes, uncovering the stories woven into its cities and towns.

SIDE EXCURSIONS: OFF THE BEATEN PATH

Embark on a journey beyond the typical ports of call, discovering hidden gems and local treasures with these off-the-beaten-path side excursions along the Rhine. we'll now navigate lesser-known destinations that promise unique experiences, cultural immersion, and a deeper connection with the enchanting landscapes of the Rhine.

Zons: Medieval Charms on the Rhine's Edge
Timewarp Town:
Venture off the main route to Zons, a medieval town frozen in time. Wander through cobblestone streets lined with half-timbered houses and visit Zonser Grind, a historic mill. Feel the medieval ambiance while exploring this well-preserved gem.

Loreley Valley: Legends and Landscapes
Mystical Vistas:
Take a detour to the Loreley Valley, a UNESCO World Heritage site known for its stunning scenery and lore. Explore the Loreley Visitor Center, delving into the legends surrounding the Loreley rock. Hike through vineyards for panoramic views of the Rhine.

Eltz Castle: A Fairytale Fortress
Castle in the Woods:
Journey to Eltz Castle, an idyllic fortress tucked away in a lush forest. Marvel at the fairytale architecture and medieval charm of this well-preserved gem. Take a guided tour to uncover the castle's rich history and intricate interiors.

Rüdesheim's Siegfried's Mechanisches Musikkabinett
Musical Marvels:
In Rüdesheim, veer off the standard path to discover Siegfried's Mechanisches Musikkabinett. This museum houses a remarkable

collection of self-playing mechanical instruments, providing a unique glimpse into the history of music automation.

Schwetzingen Palace Gardens
Baroque Beauty:
Step away from the riverbanks to visit the Schwetzingen Palace Gardens. Admire the meticulously landscaped Baroque gardens, featuring sculptures, water elements, and the charming Temple of Mercury. Immerse yourself in the serenity of this picturesque retreat.

Mannheim: Industrial Heritage
Revolutionary Relics:
Explore Mannheim's industrial heritage with a visit to the Technoseum. This museum showcases the region's industrial evolution, featuring vintage machinery, interactive exhibits, and insights into the innovation that shaped Mannheim.

Koblenz's Ehrenbreitstein Fortress
Fortress Majesty:
Opt for a journey to Ehrenbreitstein Fortress in Koblenz. Ride the cable car for breathtaking views of the confluence of the Rhine and Moselle rivers. Explore the fortress grounds, housing museums, gardens, and historical exhibitions.

Nierstein: Vineyard Exploration
Wine Country Stroll:
Head to Nierstein for a unique vineyard experience. Wander through the terraced vineyards, interact with local winemakers, and indulge in wine tastings. Gain insights into the winemaking traditions of the Rhine Valley.

Boppard's Roman Fort
Ancient Ruins:
Uncover the lesser-known history of Boppard by visiting its Roman Fort. Explore the archaeological site, featuring remnants of a Roman military camp. Immerse yourself in the Roman legacy along the Rhine.

Worms: City of Nibelungen
Epic Legends:
Detour to Worms, a city steeped in Nibelungen saga. Visit the Nibelungen Museum to explore the mythological tales and cultural significance associated with this ancient city.

Local Flavors: Culinary Experiences Off the Beaten Path
Hidden Gastronomy:
Delight your taste buds with side excursions focused on local gastronomy. From charming cafes to family-owned eateries, savor the authentic flavors of regional cuisines away from the tourist hotspots.

Uncover the allure of these off-the-beaten-path destinations, revealing the Rhine's diverse tapestry beyond the usual ports of call. Each side excursion promises a unique perspective, providing a deeper understanding of the rich history, culture, and natural wonders that grace the Rhine River's scenic route.

Chapter Five
HISTORIC LANDMARKS ALONG THE RHINE

UNESCO WORLD HERITAGE SITES

Cologne Cathedral (Cologne, Germany).

In this captivating journey through history, immerse yourself in the architectural splendor and religious significance of Cologne Cathedral. This UNESCO World Heritage Site, standing proudly along the banks of the Rhine in Cologne, Germany, boasts a rich legacy that stretches back centuries.

Gothic Grandeur:

Architectural Marvel:

Cologne Cathedral, or Kölner Dom in German, is a testament to Gothic architecture's zenith. Its construction commenced in 1248, and after a hiatus, the cathedral was completed in 1880. Its towering spires, intricate facades, and ornate details capture the essence of medieval craftsmanship.

Religious Significance:

Spiritual Heart:

The cathedral is not just an architectural masterpiece but also a symbol of spiritual significance. It houses the Shrine of the Three

Kings, believed to contain relics of the Magi who visited the infant Jesus. Pilgrims and visitors alike are drawn to the cathedral's religious aura.

Stained Glass Symphony:

Artistic Elegance:

Step inside to witness a breathtaking display of stained glass windows. The cathedral's windows depict biblical narratives, saints, and scenes from Cologne's history.

The play of light through these intricate artworks creates a mesmerizing kaleidoscope within the sacred space.

Turbulent History:

War and Restoration:

Cologne Cathedral has endured its share of challenges. During World War II, the cathedral suffered damage, but its structural resilience saved it from complete destruction. Restoration efforts post-war reaffirmed its cultural importance, leading to its UNESCO recognition in 1996.

Ascend to Awe:

Climbing the Towers:

For the adventurous at heart, a climb to the cathedral's towers offers panoramic views of Cologne and the Rhine River. The ascent involves navigating narrow staircases and takes you close to the cathedral's iconic spires. The breathtaking vistas from the top are a reward for the effort.

Cultural Icon:

Modern-Day Symbol:

Beyond its religious role, Cologne Cathedral has become an iconic symbol of the city and a UNESCO World Heritage Site. It serves as a cultural hub, hosting concerts, exhibitions, and events that celebrate its historical and artistic legacy.

Visitor Experience:

Guided Tours:

Delve deeper into the cathedral's history with guided tours that unveil hidden stories and details. Learn about the meticulous craftsmanship, the challenges faced during construction, and the cathedral's role in Cologne's identity.

Cologne's Skyline Sentinel:

Night Illumination:

As the sun sets, Cologne Cathedral becomes a radiant silhouette against the night sky. Illuminated by lights, it transforms into a captivating spectacle, casting its majestic shadow over the Rhine and becoming a beacon for residents and visitors alike.

Cologne Cathedral stands as a living testament to Cologne's resilience, faith, and artistic prowess. Its majestic spires reaching towards the heavens, intricate details telling tales of centuries past, and the spiritual aura within its walls make it an unmissable highlight along the Rhine's historic landmarks. Journey through time and architecture as you explore the enchanting Cologne Cathedral on your Rhine river cruise.

Rhine Gorge (Germany).

Embark on a visual odyssey as we explore the enchanting Rhine Gorge, a natural wonder that graces the course of the Rhine River in Germany. This captivating stretch, nestled between Bingen and Koblenz, is a testament to the harmonious dance between nature and history.

Majestic Landscapes:

Vineyard-Carpeted Hills:

The Rhine Gorge unfolds like a living tapestry, with lush vineyards carpeting the hills that embrace the meandering river. The undulating landscape, adorned with medieval castles and charming villages, creates an idyllic setting that seems straight out of a fairytale.

Iconic Castles:

Sentinels of History:

The Rhine Gorge is studded with over 40 castles and fortresses that crown the hills, each with its own tale to tell. Among them, the iconic Lorelei Rock stands tall, shrouded in myths and legends. The sight of these medieval structures transports you to a bygone era of knights, battles, and romance.

Lorelei Rock:

Siren's Song:

Lorelei Rock, a steep slate rock formation, looms over the Rhine. According to folklore, a siren named Lorelei lured sailors to their fate with her mesmerizing song.

Today, the rock stands as a symbol of both natural beauty and mythical allure, providing a stunning backdrop to your Rhine River cruise.

Vibrant Vineyards:

Wine Country Delight:

The Rhine Gorge is part of the Middle Rhine, a UNESCO World Heritage Site celebrated not only for its castles but also for its vineyards. The region is renowned for producing some of Germany's finest wines, and the terraced vineyards add a vibrant splash of green to the landscape.

Cruise Highlights:

Scenic River Cruises:

Your journey through the Rhine Gorge on a river cruise is a highlight in itself. As the boat gracefully navigates the river's twists and turns, you'll be treated to ever-changing panoramas of castles, vineyards, and charming towns.

Cultural Heritage:

Historic Towns:

Along the Rhine Gorge, encounter picturesque towns like Bacharach and St. Goar. These settlements, with their half-timbered houses and cobblestone streets, invite you to step into the past. Explore the streets, visit local shops, and soak in the atmosphere of these timeless communities.

Vantage Points:

Best Views:

For an unparalleled view of the Rhine Gorge, head to one of the many scenic vantage points. The viewpoints offer panoramic perspectives of the river, the castles, and the surrounding countryside, providing opportunities for breathtaking photos and lasting memories.

Nature's Symphony:

Seasonal Beauty:

The Rhine Gorge undergoes a magical transformation with each season. Whether adorned in the vibrant hues of spring blossoms, the lush greenery of summer, the fiery palette of autumn, or the serene winter landscapes, the gorge captivates with its ever-changing beauty.

The Rhine Gorge, with its dramatic landscapes and historical charm, is a quintessential part of any Rhine River cruise. As you meander through this natural masterpiece, let the tales of castles, the allure of Lorelei Rock, and the beauty of vineyards weave a memorable chapter into your Rhine adventure.

Strasbourg- Grande le (Strasbourg, France).

Welcome to Grande Île, the historic heart of Strasbourg, France, where the old-world charm of cobblestone streets and timber-framed houses harmonizes with the vibrant pulse of contemporary life. This UNESCO World Heritage Site is a cultural treasure trove that invites you to explore its rich history, diverse architecture, and artistic allure.

Architectural Splendors:

Half-Timbered Houses:

Grande Île is renowned for its well-preserved medieval architecture, with a particular highlight being the enchanting half-timbered houses. These structures, adorned with intricate woodwork and colorful facades, create a picturesque scene that feels straight out of a storybook.

Strasbourg Cathedral:

Gothic Grandeur:

Dominating the skyline, Strasbourg Cathedral (Cathédrale Notre-Dame de Strasbourg) is an awe-inspiring masterpiece of Gothic architecture. The cathedral's intricate façade, soaring spire, and stunning stained glass windows make it a must-visit landmark. Climb to the top for panoramic views of the city.

La Petite France:

Canals and Quaintness:

Explore the charming district of La Petite France, where canals wind their way through a maze of narrow streets. The area is characterized by its historic buildings, floral displays, and waterfront cafés, creating a serene and picturesque ambiance.

Historical Significance:

European Quarter:

As the historical center of Strasbourg, Grande Île is a testament to the city's cultural and political significance. Stroll through Place Kléber, the central square, and discover monuments that narrate the region's past, including the statue of Johannes Gutenberg.

Museums and Galleries:

Cultural Exploration:

Grande Île is home to several museums and galleries, each offering a unique perspective on Strasbourg's cultural tapestry. Visit the Strasbourg Museum of Fine Arts, Strasbourg Historical Museum, and Alsatian Museum to delve into the city's artistic and historical heritage.

Culinary Delights:

Indulge in the culinary delights of Grande Île by exploring its array of restaurants and cafés. From traditional Alsatian cuisine to international flavors, the district offers a diverse culinary journey. Enjoy a leisurely meal in a riverside bistro or savor local specialties in a historic setting.

Shopping and Markets:

Boutiques and Markets:

Grande Île invites you to indulge in retail therapy with its boutique-lined streets and bustling markets. From high-end fashion to unique artisanal finds, the district caters to a range of shopping preferences. Don't miss the Strasbourg Christmas Market if visiting during the festive season.

Cultural Events:

Festivals and Performances:

Immerse yourself in the cultural vibrancy of Grande Île by checking the local events calendar. The district hosts festivals, performances, and cultural celebrations throughout the year, offering visitors a chance to engage with the dynamic spirit of Strasbourg.

River Cruises and Views:

Grande Île is embraced by the River Ill, providing opportunities for scenic river cruises. Embark on a boat tour to admire the cityscape from a different perspective, appreciating the blend of historic and modern architecture along the water's edge.

Speyer Cathedral (Speyer, Germany).

Welcome to Speyer, Germany, where the skyline is graced by the majestic presence of Speyer Cathedral (Dom zu Speyer). This UNESCO World Heritage Site stands as a testament to the architectural prowess of the Romanesque era and invites you to explore its sacred halls and storied history.

Architectural Grandeur:
Speyer Cathedral is an exemplar of Romanesque architecture, characterized by its robust and harmonious design. The cathedral's imposing façade, intricate sculptures, and massive columns showcase the grandeur of this medieval architectural style.

Imposing Facade:

Entrance Portals:
Approach the cathedral through its intricately adorned entrance portals, each telling a visual story through detailed carvings and sculptures. The portrayal of biblical scenes and figures adds a layer of storytelling to the cathedral's exterior.

Interior Marvels:
Nave and Aisles:
Step into the cathedral's interior to marvel at the expansive nave and aisles. The Romanesque design emphasizes a sense of unity and solidity, creating a solemn atmosphere that enhances the spiritual experience for visitors.

Imperial Tombs:
Resting Royalty:
Speyer Cathedral serves as the final resting place for several German emperors, including Emperor Conrad II. The imperial tombs within the cathedral add a historical dimension, offering a glimpse into the regal legacy of Speyer.

Crypt and Treasury:
Hidden Treasures:
Descend into the cathedral's crypt, where the remains of historical figures rest in eternal peace. The treasury holds a collection of precious artifacts, including medieval manuscripts, religious relics, and ceremonial objects.

Bell Tower Views:
For panoramic views of Speyer and its surroundings, climb the cathedral's bell tower. The ascent rewards visitors with

breathtaking vistas, providing a unique perspective on the city and the Rhine region.

Historical Significance:
Symbol of Faith:
Speyer Cathedral, consecrated in 1061, holds immense historical significance as one of the largest Romanesque cathedrals in Germany. Its enduring presence symbolizes the enduring faith and cultural heritage of the region.

Festivals and Events:
Cultural Celebrations:
Experience the cathedral's vibrant cultural life by attending festivals and events hosted within its sacred walls. From religious ceremonies to musical performances, Speyer Cathedral continues to be a venue for cultural expression.

Guided Tours:
Insights from Experts:
Engage in a guided tour to gain deeper insights into the architectural nuances, historical anecdotes, and religious importance of Speyer Cathedral. Knowledgeable guides provide context that enhances the visitor experience.

Kinderdijk-Elshout (Alblasserwaard, Netherlands).

Welcome to Kinderdijk-Elshout, a mesmerizing landscape in Alblasserwaard, Netherlands, where the iconic windmills stand as silent sentinels against the backdrop of scenic waterways. Let's embark on a journey to discover the charm and heritage that make Kinderdijk-Elshout a UNESCO World Heritage Site.

Windmill Symphony:

Kinderdijk-Elshout boasts a collection of 19 well-preserved windmills, each telling a story of ingenuity and water management. The windmills, built in the 18th century, form a unique ensemble that is both visually striking and historically significant.

Water Management:

The windmills of Kinderdijk-Elshout played a crucial role in reclaiming land from the surrounding rivers and managing water levels. Explore the intricate network of canals, dikes, and pumping stations that showcase Dutch expertise in hydraulic engineering.

Picturesque Landscapes:

Reflections on Water:

Capture the postcard-perfect scenes of windmills reflected in the calm waters of the canals. Whether bathed in the warm hues of sunrise or the soft glow of sunset, Kinderdijk-Elshout is a photographer's paradise.

Historical Significance:

Cultural Heritage:

The windmills are not just functional structures; they are a testament to the Netherlands' battle against water. Learn about the history of Kinderdijk-Elshout and how these structures became a symbol of Dutch water management.

Museum Windmill:

Visit the museum windmill to get an immersive experience of life in a windmill. Explore the living quarters, witness the grinding of grain, and gain insights into the daily lives of the millers and their families.

Walking and Cycling Trails:

Wander along the well-marked trails or cycle through the meadows surrounding Kinderdijk-Elshout. The peaceful countryside offers a serene escape, allowing visitors to connect with nature while enjoying the cultural richness of the region.

Visitor Center:

Interactive Exhibits:

Enhance your understanding of Kinderdijk's UNESCO status and the ongoing efforts in water management at the Visitor Center. Interactive exhibits provide educational insights into the significance of this cultural landscape.

Festivals and Events:

Kinderdijk-Elshout comes alive during special events and festivals. Experience the vibrant atmosphere as locals and visitors gather to celebrate the rich cultural heritage of the region.

Boat Tours:

Waterborne Exploration:

Opt for a boat tour to navigate the waterways and gain a different perspective of the windmills. The gentle glide of the boat offers a tranquil experience, allowing you to appreciate the landscape from a unique vantage point.

Historic Monuments of Ancient Cologne (Cologne, Germany).

Welcome to Cologne, Germany, where the historic monuments bear witness to the city's rich and varied history. Let's embark on a virtual tour through time, exploring the UNESCO World Heritage Site – the Historic Monuments of Ancient Cologne.

Cologne Cathedral (Kölner Dom):

Gothic Grandeur:

Dominating the skyline, the Cologne Cathedral is a masterpiece of Gothic architecture. Explore the intricacies of its soaring spires, detailed façade, and awe-inspiring stained glass windows. The cathedral, a symbol of faith and engineering marvel, stands as a testament to medieval craftsmanship.

Romanesque Churches:

Spiritual Sanctuaries:

Immerse yourself in the tranquility of Cologne's Romanesque churches. From the Basilica of St. Severin to the Church of St. Gereon, each structure tells a story of religious devotion and architectural brilliance. Marvel at the frescoes, sculptures, and centuries-old mosaics that adorn these sacred spaces.

City Walls and Gates:

Explore remnants of Cologne's medieval fortifications, including sections of the city walls and gates. The Eigelsteintorburg and Hahnentor are among the surviving gate structures that once protected the city. Walk along these historic ramparts and envision Cologne's medieval defenses.

Roman Germanic Museum (Römisch-Germanisches Museum):

Archaeological Treasures:

Delve into Cologne's Roman past at the Roman Germanic Museum. Discover artifacts ranging from intricately crafted jewelry to remnants of Roman architecture. The museum provides a fascinating glimpse into the city's position as a significant Roman settlement.

Praetorium and Roman Governor's Palace:

Seat of Power:

Step into the archaeological site of the Praetorium, once the Roman Governor's Palace. Wander through the remains of grand halls, courtyards, and underground chambers. Uncover the layers of Cologne's history, from Roman rule to medieval governance.

Jewish Mikveh (Ritual Bath):

Cultural Diversity:

Visit the Mikveh, a Jewish ritual bath dating back to medieval times. This archaeological gem reflects the diversity of Cologne's historical population. Learn about the Jewish community's contributions to the city's cultural tapestry.

Historic Old Town (Altstadt):

Charming Alleys:

Stroll through the narrow alleys of Cologne's Old Town, where medieval and Renaissance buildings create a picturesque setting. The Alter Markt square, with its colorful houses and the iconic City Hall (Rathaus), invites you to soak in the ambiance of a bygone era.

Hohenzollern Bridge:

Iconic Crossing:

The Hohenzollern Bridge, adorned with love locks, spans the Rhine River. Enjoy panoramic views of the cityscape and Cologne Cathedral from this historic bridge. Join the tradition of affixing a lock to symbolize lasting love as you take in the river's gentle flow.

Upper Middle Rhine Valley_(Germany).

Welcome to the Upper Middle Rhine Valley in Germany, a UNESCO World Heritage Site renowned for its breathtaking landscapes, historic castles, and enchanting vineyards.

Loreley Rock:

Mythical Beauty:

Behold the iconic Loreley Rock, a steep slate rock on the bank of the Rhine. According to legend, a siren named Loreley lured sailors to their fate with her enchanting song. Admire the panoramic views from the viewpoint and feel the magic of this storied location.

Rhine Castles:

Sentinels of the Valley:

Discover the majesty of medieval castles perched atop vine-covered hills. Marksburg Castle, Rheinfels Castle, and Burg Katz are just a few examples that stand as silent witnesses to centuries of Rhine River history. Explore their ramparts, dungeons, and towers for a glimpse into the region's medieval past.

Vineyards and Winemaking Tradition:

Culinary Delights:

Traverse the terraced vineyards that define the Rhine's landscape. Learn about the art of winemaking from local vintners and savor the flavors of the renowned Riesling wines. The vine-clad slopes create a picturesque backdrop for wine enthusiasts and connoisseurs alike.

Rhine Gorge:

Natural Wonders:

Cruise through the Rhine Gorge, a UNESCO-listed stretch renowned for its dramatic scenery. Towering cliffs, steep vineyards, and postcard-perfect villages unfold along the riverbanks. Marvel at the geological wonders that have shaped this captivating landscape.

Medieval Towns:

Quaint Charm:

Wander through charming medieval towns like Bacharach, St. Goar, and Oberwesel. Cobblestone streets, half-timbered houses, and historic market squares transport you back in time.

Explore local shops, indulge in regional cuisine, and soak in the authentic ambiance of these well-preserved settlements.

Niederwald Monument (Niederwalddenkmal):

Symbol of Unity:

Ascend to the Niederwald Monument, a colossal statue symbolizing the reunification of Germany. Enjoy panoramic views of the Rhine Valley from this vantage point. The monument's significance extends beyond its grandeur, echoing the spirit of unity in German history.

Festivals and Traditions:

Immerse yourself in the vibrant traditions of the region by participating in local festivals. From wine festivals to medieval fairs, these events showcase the cultural richness and community spirit that thrive along the Rhine.

ICONIC CASTLES AND FORTRESSES

Marksburg Castle: A Timeless Fortress

Perched majestically on a hill overlooking the enchanting Rhine River, Marksburg Castle stands as a testament to the timeless allure of medieval fortresses. This iconic stronghold, nestled near the town of Braubach in Germany, is a treasure trove of history, offering visitors a captivating journey back to a bygone era.

A Glimpse into History:

Marksburg Castle, dating back to the 12th century, has weathered centuries of change while retaining its medieval charm. Its strategic hilltop location provided a commanding view of the Rhine Valley, making it an essential bastion for territorial defense and control of river trade routes.

Over the years, the castle witnessed the ebb and flow of power, surviving wars, sieges, and evolving political landscapes.

Architectural Marvel:

The architecture of Marksburg Castle is a masterpiece of medieval military engineering. With its sturdy walls, imposing towers, and a strategic layout designed for defense, the castle served not only as a symbol of strength but as a formidable deterrent to would-be invaders.

The labyrinthine interiors boast an array of chambers, halls, and living quarters, each echoing the stories of the past.

Life Within the Walls:

As visitors explore Marksburg Castle, they are transported into the daily life of medieval inhabitants. The Great Hall resonates with tales of feasts and celebrations, while the dungeon whispers stories of imprisonment and intrigue.

The living quarters provide a glimpse into the challenges and comforts experienced by castle residents, highlighting the resilience required for survival in an era defined by uncertainty.

Museum of Medieval Lore:

Marksburg Castle has seamlessly transformed into a living museum, preserving the rich history of the Rhine region. Exhibits within its walls showcase medieval weaponry, armor, and artifacts, offering an immersive experience for history enthusiasts.

The castle's museum not only educates but allows visitors to touch, feel, and envision the daily life of those who once called Marksburg home.

Rhine River Panorama:

One of the most enchanting features of Marksburg Castle is the panoramic view it affords of the Rhine River. The castle's strategic location not only served defensive purposes but also provided a breathtaking backdrop for those who resided within.

Today, visitors can stand on the ramparts and marvel at the same vistas that captivated medieval lords and ladies.

Preserving Heritage:

Marksburg Castle's resilience through centuries is owed in part to the efforts of preservationists and historians. Restoration projects have carefully maintained the castle's authenticity while ensuring its accessibility to modern-day admirers.

The commitment to preserving this cultural gem allows current generations to connect with the past and appreciate the architectural prowess of their forebears.

Visiting Marksburg Today:

For contemporary travelers embarking on a Rhine River cruise, Marksburg Castle beckons with its allure. The guided tours offer a blend of historical insight and captivating anecdotes, bringing the castle's stones to life.

Exploring its battlements, chambers, and courtyards, visitors can absorb the medieval ambiance and gain a profound appreciation for the enduring spirit of Marksburg.

Rheinstein Castle: Where Romance Meets Architecture

Situated atop a lush hill overlooking the picturesque Rhine River, Rheinstein Castle emerges as a true embodiment of medieval romance and architectural splendor. With its fairytale-like setting and rich history, Rheinstein Castle beckons travelers to immerse themselves in a world where tales of chivalry, love, and architectural brilliance converge.

Historical Tapestry:

Dating back to the early 14th century, Rheinstein Castle weaves a tapestry of history that resonates through the centuries. Originally constructed as a toll station for river commerce, the castle's role evolved over time, witnessing periods of expansion, decline, and restoration. Its resilient spirit mirrors the ebb and flow of the Rhine's own narrative.

Architectural Marvel:

Rheinstein Castle stands as an exquisite example of Rhine Romanticism, a movement in the 19th century that celebrated the region's medieval heritage. The castle's architecture, with its turrets, crenellated walls, and commanding towers, exudes a fairytale charm that captures the imagination. Each stone tells a story, inviting visitors to step into a realm where knights and damsels once roamed.

Knightly Resurgence:

The 19th-century restoration, led by the visionary Prince Frederick of Prussia, breathed new life into Rheinstein Castle. Inspired by the Romantic movement, Prince Frederick aimed to revive the castle's medieval glory, introducing elements like the Knights' Hall, adorned with heraldic symbols, suits of armor, and a grand fireplace. This revival not only preserved the castle but enhanced its allure.

Romantic Gardens:

Surrounding Rheinstein Castle is a lush expanse of carefully landscaped gardens, adding a touch of romanticism to the medieval ambiance. The gardens, with their vibrant blooms, winding pathways, and panoramic views of the Rhine, provide an idyllic backdrop for visitors seeking a moment of tranquility amidst the historical grandeur.

Rhine Panorama:

Perched strategically on the hillside, Rheinstein Castle offers breathtaking panoramic views of the Rhine River and its scenic surroundings. The vantage points from the castle's towers and terraces provide a mesmerizing tableau, inviting travelers to witness the meandering river, vineyard-clad hills, and charming villages that dot the landscape.

Visitor Experience:

For modern-day explorers embarking on a Rhine River cruise, Rheinstein Castle promises an enchanting experience. Guided tours lead visitors through the castle's chambers, allowing them to marvel at its architectural details, immerse themselves in its history, and savor the romance that permeates the air. The castle's well-preserved interiors and captivating exhibits ensure a memorable journey into the past.

Preserving the Past:

Rheinstein Castle's preservation is a testament to the dedication of those who recognize its historical and cultural significance. The ongoing efforts to maintain the castle's integrity while welcoming visitors underscore the importance of preserving architectural gems that bridge the gap between eras.

Burg Eltz: A Fairytale in the Eifel Forest

Nestled amidst the enchanting Eifel Forest in Germany, Burg Eltz emerges as a fairytale castle that captivates the imagination with its picturesque setting, medieval charm, and rich history. This architectural gem, surrounded by verdant woods and nestled in a serene valley, stands as a testament to the enduring allure of medieval fortresses.

A Hidden Gem:

Burg Eltz, often referred to as Eltz Castle, is renowned for its secluded location. Tucked away in the hills above the Moselle River, this hidden gem remains untouched by the passage of time. Surrounded by dense forests, the castle's spires and turrets rise above the canopy, creating a scene straight from the pages of a storybook.

Architectural Splendor:

Dating back to the 12th century, Burg Eltz showcases a remarkable blend of Romanesque, Baroque, and Gothic architectural styles. Its well-preserved structure boasts towers, courtyards, and ornate details that transport visitors to a bygone era. The castle's three main parts—Rübenach, Rodendorf, and Kempenich—are a harmonious symphony of medieval craftsmanship.

Family Heritage:

Unlike many castles that changed hands over the centuries, Burg Eltz has remained in the possession of the same family for more than 800 years. The Eltz family's commitment to preserving their ancestral home contributes to the castle's authenticity and allows visitors to experience the continuity of medieval traditions.

Magical Surroundings:

Approaching Burg Eltz is like entering a fairytale realm. The winding road through the forest unveils glimpses of the castle, gradually building anticipation.

Upon arrival, visitors are greeted by a stone bridge spanning a bubbling stream—a scene that enhances the magical atmosphere and transports them to a world where knights and dragons once roamed.

Interior Treasures:

Stepping inside Burg Eltz reveals a trove of historical treasures. The castle's chambers are adorned with period furniture, artwork, and artifacts, providing a window into medieval life.

The Knights' Hall, with its impressive timber ceiling, and the Armory, housing an extensive collection of weapons and armor, offer insights into the castle's military past.

Romantic Courtyards:

Burg Eltz features several courtyards, each with its unique charm. The Romanesque inner courtyard, the shield-shaped courtyard, and the Kempenich courtyard showcase the castle's architectural evolution.These outdoor spaces, surrounded by ivy-covered walls, provide tranquil spots for contemplation.

Panoramic Views:

Perched atop a rocky outcrop, Burg Eltz rewards visitors with panoramic views of the surrounding Eifel Forest and the meandering Elzbach River. Whether from the castle's towers or the surrounding woods, the vistas evoke a sense of awe, inviting travelers to savor the beauty of the German countryside.

Visitor Experience:

For those embarking on a journey through the Eifel region or the Moselle Valley, Burg Eltz offers an immersive and memorable experience. Guided tours provide in-depth insights into the castle's history and architecture, allowing visitors to appreciate its role as both a defensive fortress and a noble residence.

Preserving History:

Burg Eltz's commitment to preservation and conservation ensures that future generations can continue to marvel at this medieval masterpiece. The castle's enduring allure serves as a testament to the importance of safeguarding historical and cultural landmarks.

Cochem Castle: A Crown Above the Moselle

Perched majestically above the serene waters of the Moselle River, Cochem Castle stands as a regal crown adorning the picturesque landscape of the German countryside. Steeped in history and architectural grandeur, this medieval fortress invites visitors to traverse through time and immerse themselves in the captivating tales of knights, nobles, and the Moselle Valley's enchanting beauty.

Overlooking the Moselle:

Situated on a hill overlooking the meandering Moselle River, Cochem Castle commands attention with its formidable presence. The castle's vantage point provides panoramic views of the surrounding vineyards, quaint villages, and the winding river below, creating a scene of unparalleled beauty.

Architectural Splendor:

Dating back to the 11th century, Cochem Castle exhibits a harmonious blend of Romanesque and Gothic architectural styles.

Towering turrets, battlements, and a distinctly medieval silhouette characterize this historical gem. As visitors approach, they are greeted by the imposing gatehouse, setting the tone for the castle's rich history.

A Tapestry of History:

Cochem Castle's history is as captivating as its architecture. From being a royal residence to enduring destruction and restoration, the castle weaves a tapestry of tales that reflect the turbulence and resilience of the region's past. Through centuries of change, the castle has stood as a silent witness to the ebb and flow of time.

Romantic Courtyards and Gardens:

Beyond its defensive structures, Cochem Castle boasts charming courtyards and gardens that add a touch of romance to the medieval fortress. Intricately designed green spaces and well-preserved courtyards invite visitors to stroll leisurely, immersing themselves in the ambiance of a bygone era.

Wine Cellars and Tasting Rooms:

Embracing its connection to the renowned Moselle wine region, Cochem Castle features wine cellars and tasting rooms that pay homage to the area's vinicultural heritage.

Visitors can explore these atmospheric spaces, discovering the nuances of local wines and savoring the flavors that have been crafted for centuries.

Interior Treasures:

Stepping inside Cochem Castle reveals a treasure trove of period furnishings, artifacts, and historical displays. The castle's interior provides a glimpse into the lifestyles of medieval nobility, offering a fascinating journey through various chambers, halls, and living spaces.

Visitor Experience:

Cochem Castle extends a warm welcome to visitors, inviting them to explore its towers, ramparts, and hidden corners. Guided tours provide insights into the castle's past, detailing its construction, restoration, and the lives of those who once called it home. The immersive experience allows guests to forge a connection with the castle's rich heritage.

Events and Festivities:

Throughout the year, Cochem Castle hosts a variety of events and festivities that celebrate its cultural significance. From medieval-themed festivals to wine-related gatherings, these occasions allow visitors to experience the castle in a lively and interactive manner.

Ehrenbreitstein Fortress: Guardian of Koblenz

Ehrenbreitstein Fortress stands as the vigilant guardian of Koblenz, a city steeped in history and strategic importance. This formidable fortress, with its robust walls and commanding presence, has witnessed centuries of change, serving as a silent witness to the ebb and flow of time.

Strategic Stronghold:

Ehrenbreitstein Fortress has stood as a strategic stronghold for centuries, strategically positioned to oversee the meeting point of two vital waterways. Its elevated location provided a vantage point that allowed those within its walls to monitor and control traffic along the Rhine, making it a key asset in times of both peace and conflict.

Historical Tapestry:

Dating back to the 16th century, Ehrenbreitstein Fortress has played a crucial role in the region's history. From serving as a military bastion to witnessing the changing tides of political alliances, the fortress has woven itself into the tapestry of the Rhineland's rich and varied past.

Architectural Grandeur:

The fortress, with its massive stone walls and imposing towers, exudes architectural grandeur. Its design reflects a blend of military practicality and aesthetic appeal, showcasing the craftsmanship of bygone eras. Visitors are greeted by sturdy gates, ramparts, and defensive structures that hint at the fortress's former military might.

Panoramic Views:

One of the highlights of Ehrenbreitstein Fortress is the breathtaking panoramic views it offers. From its elevated position, visitors can marvel at the confluence of the Rhine and Moselle rivers, the sprawling cityscape of Koblenz, and the lush landscapes that stretch beyond.

The fortress's strategic location maximizes its potential as a vantage point for capturing the beauty of the surrounding region.

Cultural Hub:

Beyond its military significance, Ehrenbreitstein Fortress has evolved into a cultural hub. Today, it houses museums, exhibitions, and cultural events that provide insights into the region's history, art, and heritage.

Visitors can explore a myriad of exhibits that bring the past to life, offering a comprehensive understanding of the fortress's multifaceted role.

Cable Car Experience:

For a truly memorable approach to Ehrenbreitstein Fortress, visitors can embark on a scenic journey via the Koblenz Cable Car. This modern mode of transport offers a breathtaking ride across the Rhine, providing unparalleled aerial views of the fortress and its surroundings.

Events and Festivities:

Ehrenbreitstein Fortress doesn't just stand as a relic of the past; it actively engages with the present through a calendar of events and festivities. From historical reenactments to cultural celebrations, the fortress invites visitors to step back in time and partake in the vibrancy of its living history.

Visitor Experience:

Welcoming visitors with open gates, Ehrenbreitstein Fortress offers an immersive experience. Guided tours delve into its history, architectural features, and the stories embedded within its walls. The journey through its corridors and chambers allows guests to connect with the fortress on a personal level.

CHARMING RIVERSIDE TOWNS

Rüdesheim am Rhein: A Winemaker's Paradise

Rüdesheim am Rhein stands as a testament to the enchanting allure of German wine country. This charming riverside town, with its medieval charm and vineyard-covered hills, welcomes visitors to a winemaker's paradise where tradition, culture, and the art of winemaking converge.

Vineyard-Carpeted Slopes:

The defining feature of Rüdesheim's landscape is the quilt of vineyard-carpeted slopes that cascade down from the Niederwald Forest. These meticulously tended vineyards, boasting rows of Riesling and other grape varietals, contribute to the town's reputation as a wine lover's haven.

The sight of terraced vines, especially during the grape harvest season, adds a vibrant palette to the already stunning scenery.

Drosselgasse: A Medieval Delight:

At the heart of Rüdesheim lies the famous Drosselgasse, a narrow cobblestone lane lined with half-timbered houses, lively wine taverns, and boutiques.

This medieval delight is a bustling hub of activity, where the strains of traditional German music fill the air, and the aroma of local delicacies tempts passersby. It's a lively thoroughfare that encapsulates the town's convivial spirit.

Wine Tasting Adventures:

Rüdesheim is synonymous with wine, and visitors are invited to embark on a sensory journey through its many wine cellars and tasting rooms. Local vintners open their doors to enthusiasts, offering guided tours and tastings that showcase the region's diverse wine portfolio.

From crisp Rieslings to full-bodied reds, each sip tells a story of the vineyards that blanket the slopes.

Niederwald Monument: Overlooking the Beauty:

For a panoramic view of Rüdesheim and the Rhine Valley, the Niederwald Monument stands atop the hills as a symbol of German unity and a vantage point for breathtaking vistas.

The journey to the monument, whether by a leisurely hike or a scenic cable car ride, is rewarded with sweeping landscapes that capture the essence of the region.

Siebenburgenblick: A Castle with a View:

Perched high above Rüdesheim, the Siebenburgenblick offers a castle experience like no other. This medieval-inspired structure not only provides a fascinating glimpse into the past but also serves as a venue for events, weddings, and gatherings.

The castle's terrace offers a front-row seat to the unfolding drama of the Rhine's meandering course.

Loreley Visitor Center: Myth and Legend:

Rüdesheim is part of the Loreley Valley, a region steeped in myth and legend. The Loreley Visitor Center delves into the lore surrounding the fabled Loreley Rock, where mermaids were said to lure sailors to their doom.

The interactive exhibits and displays bring to life the rich tapestry of stories that have woven themselves into the cultural fabric of the Rhine.

Rhine in Flames: Spectacle of Light and Fire:

One of the most anticipated events in Rüdesheim is the Rhine in Flames festival. This annual spectacle transforms the river into a canvas of light, color, and fireworks.

As the night sky erupts in a dazzling display, visitors witness the magic of the Rhine illuminated in a breathtaking fusion of tradition and modernity.

COCHEM: A FAIRYTALE BY THE MOSELLE

Along the curves of the Moselle River, Cochem emerges as a fairytale destination, where medieval charm, vineyard-clad hills, and a storybook castle create a captivating tableau. This enchanting town, adorned with half-timbered houses and surrounded by the picturesque Moselle Valley, beckons visitors into a realm where history and beauty converge.

Reichsburg Cochem: A Crown Above the Town:

Dominating the skyline of Cochem is the Reichsburg Cochem, a medieval castle perched majestically on a hill. This crowning jewel of Cochem has witnessed centuries of history and stands as a testament to the town's resilience.

Guided tours through its halls reveal a captivating narrative of knights, royalty, and the evolution of a castle that has withstood the test of time.

Historic Old Town: Timbered Elegance:

Wandering through Cochem's historic Old Town is like stepping into a fairytale. Narrow cobblestone streets wind through a tapestry of well-preserved half-timbered houses, each one telling a story of bygone eras.

The Marktplatz, with its medieval architecture and vibrant atmosphere, serves as the heart of the town, inviting visitors to soak in its timeless ambiance.

Moselle Promenade: Riverside Serenity:

The Moselle Promenade offers a tranquil retreat along the riverbank, where visitors can stroll amidst blooming flowers and enjoy panoramic views of the Moselle.

Cafés and wine gardens along the promenade provide a perfect setting to relax, sip local wines, and savor the idyllic scenery that unfolds with each passing boat on the river.

Vineyards of Cochem: Terroir and Tradition:

Surrounding Cochem are vineyards that produce some of the finest wines in the Moselle region. The steep slopes of the vine-clad hills create a stunning backdrop, emphasizing the marriage of terroir and tradition.

Wine enthusiasts can explore local vineyards, attend tastings, and gain insights into the winemaking practices that have flourished in this region for centuries.

Eltz Castle Excursion: A Day Trip into History:

While Cochem boasts its own castle, an excursion to nearby Burg Eltz adds another layer to the fairytale experience.

This well-preserved medieval castle, nestled in a dense forest, exudes a timeless charm and invites visitors to explore its courtyards, towers, and historical treasures.

The Enderttor: A Gateway to the Past:

As part of Cochem's medieval fortifications, the Enderttor stands as a historic gateway to the town. This picturesque structure, with its tower and defensive elements, transports visitors to an era where town gates played a crucial role in protecting the inhabitants.

Bacharach: Where History Meets Riverside Tranquility

Situated on the banks of the Rhine, Bacharach unfolds as a charming tapestry where history, architecture, and the serene flow of the river converge.

This picturesque town, with its well-preserved medieval structures and vineyard-covered hills, invites visitors to step back in time while immersing themselves in the tranquil beauty of its surroundings.

Alte Haus: A Glimpse into the Past:

At the heart of Bacharach's Old Town stands the Alte Haus, a timber-framed jewel dating back to the 14th century. This iconic structure, with its distinctive architecture and ornate details, offers a captivating glimpse into the town's medieval history. The

Alte Haus stands as a testament to the enduring charm of Bacharach.

Stahleck Castle: Guardian of the Rhine:

Perched on a hill overlooking Bacharach, Stahleck Castle stands as a sentinel guarding the Rhine. Originally constructed in the 12th century, this castle has witnessed centuries of history.

Today, it serves as a youth hostel, allowing visitors to not only explore its historic halls but also savor panoramic views of the Rhine Valley.

Wine Tasting in Bacharach: A Toast to the Rhine:

Bacharach's location in the heart of the Middle Rhine wine region makes it a haven for wine enthusiasts. The town is surrounded by vineyards that produce the renowned Riesling grape.

Local wine taverns, known as Weinstuben, offer the perfect setting to sample the region's wines, each sip echoing the terroir of the Rhine Valley.

Rheinsteig Trail: Hiking Amidst Vineyards:

For those seeking an active exploration, the Rheinsteig Trail provides a scenic trek through vineyards and along the Rhine. This hiking trail offers breathtaking views of the river, the town, and the surrounding landscape, allowing visitors to connect with the natural beauty that defines Bacharach.

Rhine Promenade: Riverside Serenity:

The Rhine Promenade beckons visitors to unwind along the riverbank, offering panoramic views of passing boats and the distant hills. Cafés and restaurants line the promenade, creating a tranquil setting to enjoy local cuisine while savoring the ever-changing scenery of the Rhine.

Postenturm: Tower with a View:

The Postenturm, a medieval tower, stands as a testament to Bacharach's historical fortifications. Climbing to the top rewards visitors with a panoramic view of the town, the Rhine, and the surrounding vineyards. It's a journey through time coupled with a breathtaking vantage point.

COLMAR: ALSATIAN ELEGANCE ON THE RHINE

Situated along the enchanting banks of the Rhine, Colmar emerges as a jewel of Alsace, weaving together medieval charm, vibrant colors, and a rich cultural tapestry. This Alsatian town, resembling a storybook setting, invites travelers to step into a world where cobblestone streets, half-timbered houses, and flower-laden canals create an atmosphere of timeless elegance.

La Petite Venise: A Canal-Crossed Delight:

Colmar's enchanting quarter, La Petite Venise, captures the essence of a waterborne fairytale. Quaint canals, lined with colorful buildings adorned with blooming flowers, crisscross the district. A leisurely boat ride along these canals unveils the town's picturesque beauty, reminiscent of Venice's charm.

Maison Pfister: A Renaissance Gem:

The Maison Pfister, a masterpiece of Renaissance architecture, stands proudly in Colmar's Old Town. Dating back to the 16th century, this ornate house with its richly decorated façade is a testament to the town's historical significance. Visitors can explore its interior, adorned with period furnishings, and gain insight into Colmar's past.

Unterlinden Museum: Art Amidst History:

For art aficionados, the Unterlinden Museum is a cultural haven. Housed in a former convent, the museum showcases a remarkable collection of medieval and Renaissance art.

Its centerpiece, the Isenheim Altarpiece by Matthias Grünewald, is a masterpiece that captivates with its emotional depth and intricate details.

Old Customs House: A Blend of Styles:

The Koifhus, or Old Customs House, stands as a testament to Colmar's role as a bustling trading hub. With its fusion of Gothic and Renaissance architecture, this historic building served as a meeting place for merchants. Today, it continues to charm visitors with its unique blend of architectural styles.

Covered Market: Culinary Delights of Alsace:

Colmar's Covered Market, or Marché Couvert, entices visitors with the flavors of Alsace. The market, housed in a Neo-Baroque building, is a gastronomic haven where local vendors showcase regional delicacies, including Alsatian wines, cheeses, and pastries. It's a feast for the senses in the heart of Colmar.

Bartholdi Museum: Celebrating a Visionary:

Dedicated to the town's renowned sculptor, Frédéric Auguste Bartholdi, the Bartholdi Museum offers a glimpse into his life and works. Bartholdi, best known for creating the Statue of Liberty, hailed from Colmar, and the museum pays homage to his artistic legacy.

Koblenz: The Confluence of History and Modernity

Nestled at the confluence of the Rhine and Moselle rivers, Koblenz stands as a testament to the harmonious blend of history and modernity. This German gem unfolds its charm with a rich tapestry of ancient architecture, cultural treasures, and a vibrant contemporary spirit.

Deutsches Eck: The German Corner:

At the heart of Koblenz lies the Deutsches Eck, or German Corner, where the Rhine and Moselle converge. This iconic headland features the imposing equestrian statue of Emperor William I, symbolizing the unification of Germany. The panoramic views from this point offer a breathtaking panorama of the two majestic rivers.

Koblenz Cable Car: A Sky-High Experience:

For a unique perspective of Koblenz, take a ride on the Koblenz Cable Car. Connecting the German Corner to the Ehrenbreitstein Fortress, this cable car journey provides a bird's-eye view of the city, the rivers, and the surrounding landscapes. It's an exhilarating experience that bridges the historic and modern facets of Koblenz.

Ehrenbreitstein Fortress: Guardian of the Rhine:

Perched high above the Rhine on the opposite bank, the Ehrenbreitstein Fortress stands as a guardian overlooking Koblenz. With roots dating back to the Roman era, this formidable fortress offers not only a glimpse into military history but also panoramic views of the city and river valleys below.

Old Town: Cobblestone Charms:

Koblenz's Old Town, with its narrow cobblestone streets and charming squares, is a journey through time. Explore the Florinsmarkt, where the Liebfrauenkirche (Church of Our Lady) and the Altes Kaufhaus (Old Merchant's House) grace the surroundings. Cafés, boutiques, and historic landmarks create an inviting atmosphere.

St. Castor's Basilica: A Romanesque Marvel:

St. Castor's Basilica, a masterpiece of Romanesque architecture, adds to Koblenz's cultural allure. Dating back over a millennium, this basilica is known for its crypt, ancient frescoes, and the Romanesque "Golden Virgin" statue. It's a place where the sacred and historical seamlessly intertwine.

German Corner Festivals: Celebrating Diversity:

Throughout the year, Koblenz hosts vibrant festivals at the German Corner. From wine festivals to cultural celebrations, these events showcase the city's lively spirit. Joining in the festivities provides a glimpse into the contemporary energy that pulses through Koblenz's historic veins.

Heidelberg: Scholarly Splendor on the River Neckar

Heidelberg emerges as a city of scholarly grandeur and timeless beauty. Renowned for its prestigious university, historic architecture, and poetic ambiance, Heidelberg beckons visitors to delve into a world where academic excellence and cultural richness converge.

Heidelberg Castle: A Majestic Sentinel:

Dominating the city's skyline, Heidelberg Castle stands as a majestic sentinel overlooking the River Neckar. This iconic castle, with its Gothic and Renaissance elements, tells tales of centuries past. The Great Barrel, a colossal wine vat within, adds a touch of medieval extravagance to the castle's allure.

Old Bridge (Alte Brücke): Connecting History:

Spanning the River Neckar, the Old Bridge, or Alte Brücke, is a picturesque link between Heidelberg's Old Town and the Neuenheim district. Dating back to the 18th century, this iconic bridge invites leisurely strolls, offering breathtaking views of the castle and the cityscape.

Philosopher's Walk: Contemplative Heights:

For a scenic escape, the Philosopher's Walk, or Philosophenweg, provides a vantage point above Heidelberg. This hillside path, favored by scholars and thinkers throughout history, offers panoramic views of the city, the river, and the castle. It's a place where contemplation meets natural beauty.

Heidelberg University: Academic Elegance:

Heidelberg's renowned university, founded in 1386, adds an air of academic elegance to the city. The Old University Building, adorned with a charming Renaissance facade, stands as a testament to the institution's historical significance. The university's influence on Heidelberg's cultural and intellectual identity is palpable.

Marketplace and Old Town Square: Vibrant Gathering Spaces:

Heidelberg's Marketplace, or Marktplatz, and the nearby Old Town Square (Kornmarkt) are vibrant hubs of activity. Lined with charming cafes, historic buildings, and the Church of the Holy Spirit, these squares are where the pulse of Heidelberg's daily life beats. Street performers, local markets, and cultural events often unfold in these lively spaces.

Neckar River Cruise: Scenic Waterway Exploration:

Embarking on a Neckar River cruise unveils Heidelberg's beauty from a different perspective. Drift along the river, passing beneath ancient bridges and alongside verdant landscapes. The leisurely pace of a river cruise allows for a tranquil appreciation of Heidelberg's architectural treasures along the waterfront.

Heidelberg's Student Kiss (Studentenkuß): Sweet Traditions:

Indulge in Heidelberg's sweet traditions by savoring the iconic "Heidelberg Student Kiss." This chocolate-covered marzipan treat, often exchanged as a symbol of affection, encapsulates the city's romantic allure and sweet indulgences.

VISITING CHARMING VILLAGES

Zons: A Living Medieval Town

Zons emerges as a living testament to medieval charm and a journey back in time. This enchanting village, with its well-preserved architecture, cobbled streets, and historical ambiance, invites visitors to wander through the pages of history and experience the magic of a bygone era.

Historical Roots:

Zons, with its origins dating back to the 12th century, exudes a palpable sense of history. Originally established as a toll collection point, the village flourished as a bustling center for trade and commerce during the medieval period. Today, it stands as a remarkably preserved relic of the past.

Fortified Walls and Towers:

One of Zons' defining features is its remarkably intact medieval fortifications. The village is enclosed by well-preserved walls and watchtowers, providing a glimpse into the defensive architecture of the Middle Ages. Walking along these walls offers panoramic views of the surrounding landscapes and the Rhine River.

Rheintor: Gateway to the Past:

At the heart of Zons stands Rheintor, a majestic gate that served as the main entrance to the village. This well-preserved medieval gate, crowned with a conical roof, transports visitors into the village's historical embrace. Rheintor stands as a symbol of Zons' significance as a trading hub and its resilience through centuries.

Half-Timbered Houses: Architectural Marvels:

Zons is adorned with a collection of picturesque half-timbered houses, each telling its own story of medieval craftsmanship. The intricate designs and timber detailing showcase the artistry of the builders from centuries past.Strolling through the narrow streets, visitors are immersed in the architectural elegance of a bygone era.

St. Martinus Church: Spiritual Heritage:

The St. Martinus Church, a prominent landmark in Zons, reflects the spiritual heritage of the village. With its Gothic architecture and serene atmosphere, the church provides a quiet sanctuary amidst the historical hustle and bustle. The churchyard, with ancient tombstones, adds a contemplative touch to the visit.

Marketplace and Guild Houses: Central Hub of Activity:

Zons' marketplace, surrounded by charming guild houses, was once the bustling center of medieval commerce. Today, it retains its role as a central hub of activity. The marketplace hosts events, markets, and gatherings, offering a vibrant space for locals and visitors alike.

Cultural Events and Festivals: Celebrating Tradition:

Zons comes alive with cultural events and festivals that celebrate its rich tradition. Whether it's a medieval fair, a historical reenactment, or a traditional festival, these events provide an immersive experience into Zons' lively past. Visitors have the opportunity to witness medieval customs and traditions brought to life.

Bacharach: A Medieval Jewel

Nestled in the heart of the Rhine Gorge, Bacharach stands as a medieval jewel, captivating visitors with its timeless charm and rich history. This picturesque town, surrounded by vineyards and overlooking the Rhine River, transports travelers to an era of knights, legends, and architectural splendor.

Historical Tapestry:

Bacharach's history unfolds like a captivating tapestry, woven with threads of medieval tales and historical significance. Its roots trace back over a thousand years, and the town has witnessed the ebb and flow of time, from the medieval period through the Renaissance to the present day.

Stahleck Castle: Guardian of the Heights:

Perched on the hills overlooking Bacharach, Stahleck Castle stands as a guardian of the town and a testament to medieval fortification. Originally built in the 12th century, the castle has evolved over time and today houses a youth hostel. The panoramic views from the castle offer a breathtaking panorama of the Rhine Valley.

Half-Timbered Houses: Architectural Elegance:

Bacharach's streets are lined with impeccably preserved half-timbered houses, each telling a story of craftsmanship and tradition. These charming structures, with their timber frames and intricate designs, create a postcard-perfect backdrop for exploring the town. Wandering through the cobblestone streets feels like stepping into a medieval fairy tale.

Wernerkapelle: A Testament of Love and Tragedy:

The Wernerkapelle, a small chapel overlooking Bacharach, adds a touch of romance and tragedy to the town's narrative. Legend has it that the chapel was built in memory of a young nobleman, Werner, who fell in love with a common girl.

The tragic tale is depicted in paintings within the chapel, adding an emotional layer to Bacharach's history.

Alte Haus: A Historic Residence:

The Alte Haus, or Old House, stands as one of the oldest and most remarkable buildings in Bacharach. Dating back to the 14th century, this well-preserved structure is a prime example of medieval architecture. Its stepped gables and wooden beams exemplify the town's commitment to preserving its heritage.

Marketplace and Wine Culture:

Bacharach's marketplace, surrounded by cafes and charming shops, is a lively hub of activity. The town's connection to wine culture is evident, with vineyards gracing the surrounding hills. Visitors can sample local wines, taking in the flavors of the region while enjoying the medieval ambiance of the marketplace.

Cultural Events and Festivals: Celebrating Heritage:

Bacharach comes alive with cultural events and festivals that celebrate its medieval heritage. From medieval markets to wine festivals, these events create a festive atmosphere that invites both locals and visitors to partake in the town's rich traditions.

Assmannshausen: A Wine Lover's Haven

Assmannshausen stands as a picturesque village that beckons wine enthusiasts with its rich viticultural heritage. Renowned for its exceptional red wines and charming riverside ambiance, Assmannshausen is a haven for those seeking a delightful blend of wine culture and scenic beauty.

Vineyards Painted in Red:

Assmannshausen is celebrated for its red wine, particularly the Spätburgunder (Pinot Noir), which thrives in the region's favorable climate and soil conditions. The vineyard-covered hills surrounding the village create a mesmerizing landscape, especially when the vines are laden with ripe grapes, painting the scenery in hues of green and red.

Höllenberg: The Prestigious Vineyard:

Among the vineyards gracing the hills, Höllenberg stands out as a prestigious site known for producing some of the finest red wines in the region.

The terraced slopes of Höllenberg provide an ideal environment for the cultivation of Spätburgunder grapes, contributing to the village's reputation as a wine connoisseur's destination.

Weingut Krone: A Wine Experience:

Weingut Krone, a renowned winery in Assmannshausen, invites visitors to indulge in a captivating wine experience. With a history dating back centuries, this family-owned winery not only produces exceptional wines but also offers guided tours and tastings.

The cellars, filled with oak barrels and the aroma of aging wines, provide a glimpse into the winemaking traditions of the region.

Assmannshäuser Höllenberg Wine Festival: A Toast to Tradition:

The Assmannshäuser Höllenberg Wine Festival, held annually, is a lively celebration that brings together locals and visitors alike. Against the backdrop of the Rhine River, the festival showcases the village's wine culture with tastings, live music, and cultural performances. It's a joyous occasion that reflects the community's pride in its winemaking heritage.

Historic Charm Along the Riverfront:

The village itself exudes historic charm, especially along the riverfront where timber-framed houses, adorned with colorful flowers, line the streets. The rhythmic flow of the Rhine adds a soothing soundtrack to leisurely strolls along the waterfront. Quaint cafes and wine bars invite visitors to savor local vintages while enjoying panoramic views of the river.

Niederwald Monument: Guardian of the Vineyards:

Perched above Assmannshausen, the Niederwald Monument watches over the vineyards and the village. This colossal statue, representing the unity of the German Empire, offers not only historical significance but also panoramic vistas of the Rhine Valley. The journey to the monument, whether by foot or the Niederwald Cable Car, adds an adventurous touch to the visit.

Rüdesheim: Where Wine and Tradition Meet

Rüdesheim stands as a captivating testament to the harmonious blend of wine culture and centuries-old traditions. This charming town, adorned with cobblestone streets and historic architecture, beckons travelers to embark on a sensory journey where the aroma of fine wines mingles with the echoes of folklore.

Drosselgasse: The Iconic Alley of Life:

Central to Rüdesheim's charm is the lively Drosselgasse, a narrow alley brimming with life and cultural vibrancy. Lined with charming wine taverns, boutiques, and open-air cafes, Drosselgasse is the pulse of Rüdesheim's social scene.

Visitors can immerse themselves in the convivial atmosphere, where the clinking of glasses and the melodies of live music create an unforgettable ambiance.

Siegfried's Mechanical Music Cabinet: A Symphony of Curiosities:

A visit to Rüdesheim wouldn't be complete without exploring Siegfried's Mechanical Music Cabinet. Housed in a 15th-century knight's tower, this whimsical museum showcases a fascinating collection of self-playing musical instruments.

The melodic tunes, emanating from intricately crafted music boxes and automated instruments, transport visitors to a bygone era of musical enchantment.

Wine Tasting at Rüdesheimer Schloss: A Toast to Tradition:

Rüdesheimer Schloss, a picturesque castle overlooking the vine-covered hills, invites wine enthusiasts to indulge in tastings of the region's renowned Riesling wines.

The castle's historic wine cellar, adorned with oak barrels and illuminated by candlelight, provides an intimate setting for savoring the flavors of Rüdesheim's terroir.

The Niederwald Monument: A Panoramic Spectacle:

For panoramic views of Rüdesheim and the Rhine Valley, a journey to the Niederwald Monument is a must. Whether ascending via the Niederwald Cable Car or hiking through the vineyards, the monument offers breathtaking vistas. The colossal statue, representing German unity, stands as a guardian over the town and the meandering Rhine River.

Ehrenfels Castle: A Ruin with a Story:

The ruins of Ehrenfels Castle, perched on the hillside overlooking Rüdesheim, add a touch of medieval allure to the landscape. The castle's storied history, coupled with its strategic position along the Rhine, sparks the imagination and invites contemplation of times gone by.

Rüdesheimer Coffee: A Local Culinary Delight:

No visit to Rüdesheim is complete without savoring a cup of Rüdesheimer Coffee. This local specialty, blending Asbach Uralt brandy, coffee, and whipped cream, is both a delightful beverage and a cultural experience. Cafes along Drosselgasse are perfect venues to relish this signature drink.

Cochem: Fairytale Setting on the Moselle River

Situated along the meandering curves of the Moselle River, Cochem emerges as a fairytale destination, adorned with a picturesque landscape, a medieval castle, and charming half-timbered houses. This enchanting town, framed by vineyard-covered hills, invites travelers to step into a storybook setting where history and natural beauty intertwine.

Reichsburg Cochem: A Castle in the Clouds:

Dominating the skyline of Cochem is the Reichsburg Cochem, a medieval castle perched majestically on a hill. Dating back to the 11th century, this fortress offers not only a glimpse into the region's history but also panoramic views of the Moselle Valley.

Visitors can embark on a guided tour to explore the castle's richly decorated rooms, medieval weaponry, and the breathtaking vantage points overlooking the town.

Moselle Promenade: Strolls by the River:

The Moselle Promenade is the heartbeat of Cochem, where the gentle flow of the river complements the charming architecture lining its banks. Taking a leisurely stroll along this riverside path provides a tranquil experience, with opportunities to enjoy cafes, boutiques, and the serene atmosphere of the Moselle.

Historical Old Town: Half-Timbered Elegance:

Cochem's Old Town transports visitors back in time with its well-preserved medieval architecture. Half-timbered houses, adorned with colorful facades and flower-filled window boxes, create a delightful backdrop for exploration.

The Marktplatz (Market Square) stands at the heart of the Old Town, surrounded by historic buildings and the impressive Baroque Martinskirche (St. Martin's Church).

Must-See Landmarks: A Tapestry of Heritage:

Aside from the Reichsburg, Cochem boasts several other landmarks that weave a tapestry of its rich heritage. The Enderttor (Endert Gate) and the Balduin Gate, remnants of the town's medieval fortifications, offer glimpses into Cochem's past. The historic Martinstor (Martin's Gate) also stands as a testament to the town's medieval defenses.

Wine Tasting in Cochem: Savoring Local Delights:

The vineyards surrounding Cochem produce some of the finest Riesling wines, and a visit to the local wine cellars provides an opportunity to savor these regional delights.

Cochem's wine culture, deeply rooted in the hillsides along the Moselle, is a vital part of the town's identity, and wine enthusiasts can indulge in tastings while enjoying scenic views of the river.

Chapter Six
SCENIC BEAUTY
BREATHTAKING LANDSCAPES

Embarking on a Rhine River cruise is not merely a journey; it's a voyage through landscapes that redefine the concept of scenic beauty. The river's meandering course unveils a tapestry of nature's grandeur, cultural richness, and historical significance. Here, every bend in the river introduces travelers to breathtaking vistas that linger in the memory long after the voyage concludes.

Vineyard-Covered Hills: A Symphony of Green and Gold:

As the cruise winds through the Upper Middle Rhine Valley, passengers are treated to an awe-inspiring sight—the verdant hills adorned with meticulously manicured vineyards.

The play of sunlight on the undulating landscapes paints a canvas of green and gold, creating a spectacle that epitomizes the romance of the Rhine. This region, celebrated for its wine production, is a living testament to the harmonious coexistence of nature and viticulture.

Rhine Gorge: Majestic Cliffs and Legendary Lore:

Navigating the Rhine Gorge is a journey into the realm of legends. Towering cliffs, adorned with medieval castles, watch over the river like silent sentinels of history.

The Lorelei Rock, shrouded in mythical tales, stands as a focal point. As the cruise glides past this iconic site, passengers are immersed in the captivating lore that has echoed through centuries, adding an extra layer of enchantment to the already mesmerizing landscape.

Quaint Villages and Riverside Towns: Picturesque Perfection:

The banks of the Rhine are studded with charming villages and towns, each exuding its own unique charm. From the half-timbered houses of Bacharach to the medieval allure of Oberwesel, every stop along the way unveils a postcard-perfect scene.

The juxtaposition of historical architecture against the backdrop of the river creates a visual symphony, captivating travelers with the quintessential charm of Rhineland.

Majestic Castles: Sentinels of a Bygone Era:

The Rhine's legendary castles perch atop hills, seemingly untouched by the passage of time. Cruising past these medieval fortresses, including Marksburg, Rheinstein, and Pfalzgrafenstein, transports passengers to an era of knights, nobility, and romanticism.

The castles, often shrouded in mist or bathed in the warm glow of the setting sun, add a magical aura to the already stunning scenery.

Panoramic Views from the Deck: A Front-Row Seat to Nature's Symphony:

The expansive decks of the cruise ship serve as a front-row seat to nature's grand symphony. Passengers can savor the ever-changing panoramas as the ship glides along the river.

From sunrise to sunset, the interplay of light and shadow on the water and the surrounding landscapes creates a cinematic experience, offering a visual feast that transcends description.

FLORA AND FAUNA OF THE RHINE VALLEY

The Rhine Valley is not only a canvas of cultural richness and historic treasures but also a sanctuary of diverse flora and fauna. As the river meanders through picturesque landscapes, it cradles a vibrant ecosystem that adds another layer of enchantment to the Rhine River cruise experience.

Floral Symphony Along the Banks:

The banks of the Rhine River are adorned with a rich tapestry of flora, creating a visual feast for travelers. Lush vineyards blanket the hillsides, offering a verdant panorama that changes with the seasons.

Spring brings a burst of color as wildflowers carpet the meadows, while autumn transforms the landscape into a mosaic of reds, yellows, and oranges as vine leaves change hues. Each stretch of the river unveils a new botanical spectacle, making the journey a continuous immersion in nature's ever-changing beauty.

Riverside Orchards and Gardens:

As the cruise navigates through the Rhine Valley, passengers are treated to the sight of riverside orchards and gardens. Fruit-bearing trees, including apple and cherry varieties, thrive in this fertile region. The carefully cultivated gardens of historic castles and estates add a touch of elegance, creating a harmonious blend of nature and human ingenuity.

Avian Ballet in the Skies:

The Rhine Valley is a haven for birdwatchers, with a diverse avian population soaring through the skies. Kingfishers, herons, and swans are a common sight, while birds of prey, such as eagles and falcons, add a majestic touch to the aerial ballet.

The riparian habitats along the riverbanks provide an ideal environment for various bird species, making the cruise a delight for nature enthusiasts and bird lovers.

Aquatic Life Beneath the Surface:

Beneath the Rhine's sparkling surface lies a world of aquatic wonders. The river supports a variety of fish species, including trout, salmon, and perch.

Additionally, the Rhine is home to freshwater mussels, contributing to the overall biodiversity of the ecosystem. The clear waters allow passengers to catch glimpses of these underwater inhabitants, enhancing the immersive nature experience.

Cultural Influence on the Landscape:

Human cultivation and settlement along the Rhine have not only shaped the cultural landscape but also influenced the region's flora.

Terraced vineyards, meticulously maintained gardens, and carefully landscaped castle grounds showcase the symbiotic relationship between human activity and the natural environment. The blend of cultural and natural elements creates a captivating tableau that unfolds with every passing mile.

PHOTOGRAPHY TIPS FOR CAPTURING THE BEAUTY

Embarking on a Rhine River cruise offers a visual feast of cultural landmarks, scenic landscapes, and charming villages. To ensure you capture the essence and beauty of this enchanting journey, consider these photography tips:

Golden Hour Magic:

Seize the magical moments during the golden hours—shortly after sunrise and before sunset. The soft, warm glow enhances the beauty of the landscapes, castles, and riverside scenes. Experiment with long shadows and captivating silhouettes to add drama to your images.

Iconic Castle Perspectives:

Capture the grandeur of Rhine's iconic castles by seeking unique perspectives. Experiment with angles, framing, and focal lengths to create captivating compositions. Consider the play of light and shadows on the castle walls during different times of the day for diverse visual effects.

Reflections on the Water:

Utilize the reflective surfaces of the Rhine River to enhance your compositions. Calm mornings or evenings provide ideal conditions for capturing mirror-like reflections of castles, villages, and the surrounding landscapes. Incorporate reflections to add depth and symmetry to your photographs.

Vibrant Riverside Villages:

The charming villages along the Rhine are a treasure trove of picturesque scenes. Capture the colorful facades, cobblestone streets, and lively atmospheres. Engage with local life to document candid moments, such as locals enjoying their day or traditional festivities.

Framing with Foliage:

Enhance your compositions by framing key subjects with natural elements. Utilize overhanging branches, vibrant flowers, or architectural elements to create a sense of depth and context. Framing adds visual interest and guides the viewer's focus to the main subject.

Candid Cultural Moments:

Immerse yourself in the local culture and capture candid moments that tell a story. Whether it's a street performer, a bustling market, or locals engaging in daily activities, candid shots convey the authentic spirit of the places you visit.

Navigating the Waters:

Capture the essence of river travel by focusing on the cruise experience itself. Document the ship navigating the river, fellow passengers enjoying the views, and crew members at work.

Include shots of the cruise ship against the backdrop of scenic landscapes for a comprehensive visual narrative.

Nighttime Wonders:

Experiment with nighttime photography to capture the Rhine under a starry sky or the beautifully illuminated castles and villages. Use a tripod for stability and extended exposure times. Leverage the ship's deck for a unique vantage point.

Details and Textures:

Zoom in on the intricate details of castles, architectural elements, or cultural artifacts. Capture textures, patterns, and close-ups to add depth and interest to your visual storytelling.

Macro shots of local cuisine, crafts, or unique features offer intimate glimpses into the destination's character.

Editing Magic:

Post-processing can elevate your images. Experiment with editing tools to enhance colors, contrast, and sharpness. Consider converting some images to black and white for a timeless feel, especially for capturing the historic ambiance of the castles.

Remember to balance capturing memories with experiencing the journey. Whether you're a photography enthusiast or a casual shooter, these tips will help you create a visual diary that encapsulates the allure of a Rhine River cruise.

NATURE RESERVES AND WILDLIFE

Nature Reserves Along the Rhine

Embarking on a Rhine River cruise unveils not only the architectural wonders of historic castles and charming villages but also the natural splendor preserved within the region's nature reserves.

As you traverse the Rhine, you'll encounter several areas dedicated to conserving the unique flora and fauna that contribute to the ecological richness of this iconic river. Here's a glimpse into the nature reserves along the Rhine:

Drachenfels Nature Reserve:

Nestled along the Siebengebirge mountain range, the Drachenfels Nature Reserve is a haven for nature enthusiasts. Towering over the Rhine, the Drachenfels (Dragon's Rock) provides panoramic views of the river.

The reserve is home to diverse plant species, and hiking trails offer an opportunity to witness the region's natural beauty.

Rhine Gorge Nature Reserve:

Recognized as a UNESCO World Heritage Site, the Rhine Gorge Nature Reserve is a testament to the Rhine's geological history.

Cruise through this stunning stretch, flanked by vineyards and steep cliffs, to appreciate the diverse landscapes and unique rock formations.

Taunus Nature Park:

Spanning a significant portion of the Taunus mountain range, this nature park introduces travelers to lush forests, rolling hills, and meandering streams.

The park's biodiversity includes a variety of bird species, making it a delight for birdwatchers and those seeking tranquility in a natural setting.

Kaiserstuhl Nature Reserve:

Situated near the city of Freiburg, the Kaiserstuhl Nature Reserve is renowned for its volcanic landscapes and vibrant flora.

Orchards, vineyards, and meadows create a patchwork of colors, making it a picturesque destination. The reserve is home to rare plant species adapted to the volcanic soil.

Rhine-Taunus Nature Park:

Encompassing the Taunus and Hunsrück regions, this nature park offers a mosaic of landscapes, from dense forests to meadows.

Along the Rhine, explore the wetlands that provide habitat for various bird species. The park's trails invite visitors to immerse themselves in the serenity of the Rhine's natural surroundings.

Hegau Volcanic Region:

Venture into the Hegau Volcanic Region, where remnants of ancient volcanoes define the landscape. The Hegau region is known for its volcanic cones, lakes, and lush greenery.

Nature trails wind through this unique terrain, offering an opportunity to connect with the earth's geological history.

Mittelrhein-Klettersteig:

For adventurous souls, the Mittelrhein-Klettersteig is a via ferrata trail that combines thrilling climbs with stunning views.

As you ascend, take in the natural beauty of the Rhine Valley. The trail is designed for those seeking an active exploration of the river's surroundings.

Aargau Jura Park:

Crossing into Switzerland, the Aargau Jura Park invites cruisers to discover the Swiss part of the Rhine.

The park showcases the diverse landscapes of the Aargau Jura region, with limestone formations, dense forests, and meadows.

It's a haven for wildlife, and nature enthusiasts can spot various species in their natural habitat.

Hunsrück-Hochwald National Park:

Situated on the upper reaches of the Nahe River, this national park introduces visitors to unspoiled nature. Ancient beech forests, clear streams, and rugged landscapes create an immersive experience. Guided tours provide insights into the park's ecology and the importance of preserving its pristine condition.

Siefenklamm Nature Reserve:

This hidden gem in the Siebengebirge mountains features a picturesque gorge with a cascading stream. The Siefenklamm Nature Reserve offers a refreshing retreat into nature, and well-maintained trails guide visitors through the lush surroundings.

As you journey along the Rhine, these nature reserves not only contribute to the ecological balance of the region but also offer travelers an opportunity to reconnect with the natural world.

Whether you're an avid nature lover or simply appreciate the beauty of unspoiled landscapes, the Rhine's nature reserves provide a tranquil backdrop to your cruise experience.

The Rhine Gorge: A Natural Wonderland

The Rhine Gorge, often referred to as the "Upper Middle Rhine Valley," is a captivating stretch of the Rhine River that winds its way through Germany. This UNESCO World Heritage Site, renowned for its stunning landscapes, historic castles, and vineyard-clad hills, presents a natural wonderland that enchants every traveler embarking on a Rhine River cruise.

Geological Marvels:

The Rhine Gorge owes its dramatic appearance to a geological phenomenon known as the Rhine Graben, a rift valley formed millions of years ago. Towering cliffs and rocky outcrops tell the story of the Earth's shifting plates, creating a visually stunning landscape that captivates all who cruise through this natural wonder.

Vineyard-Covered Slopes:

The hills flanking the Rhine Gorge are adorned with meticulously terraced vineyards, a testament to the region's rich winemaking tradition. The combination of fertile soils and a favorable climate has turned this stretch of the Rhine into a renowned wine-producing area.

Visitors are treated to breathtaking views of neatly arranged vines, creating a patchwork of greenery against the river backdrop.

Romantic Castles:

Perched atop the hills like silent sentinels, medieval castles add a fairytale charm to the Rhine Gorge. Icons such as Marksburg Castle and Rheinfels Castle transport travelers back in time, offering a glimpse into the region's rich history of knights, battles, and medieval romance. Each castle has its own story to tell, contributing to the enchantment of the gorge.

Lorelei Rock:

One of the most iconic features of the Rhine Gorge is the Lorelei Rock, a steep, 433-foot high slate rock that juts into the river.

Wrapped in legend and folklore, the Lorelei has been a muse for poets and musicians throughout history.

According to myth, a siren named Lorelei would lure sailors to their doom with her enchanting song, adding an air of mystery to this natural landmark.

Diverse Flora and Fauna:

The Rhine Gorge is not just a feast for the eyes but also a haven for biodiversity. Lush vegetation along the riverbanks supports a variety of plant and animal species.

As you cruise through this natural wonderland, you may spot eagles soaring above, herons wading in the shallows, and a myriad of wildflowers dotting the landscape.

The Lorelei Song:

The cultural significance of the Rhine Gorge is further heightened by the Lorelei Song. Inspired by the mythical Lorelei and her haunting song, this German folk song adds a poetic soundtrack to the journey through the gorge. Travelers often find themselves immersed in the melodies that echo through the valleys.

Seasonal Splendors:

The Rhine Gorge undergoes a magical transformation with each season. In spring, blossoming flowers carpet the hills, while summer brings vibrant greenery and lively vineyards. Autumn paints the landscape in warm hues, and winter adds a touch of tranquility, turning the gorge into a serene winter wonderland.

Romantic Rhine Cruises:

Navigating the Rhine Gorge on a river cruise is a romantic experience that allows travelers to fully appreciate its natural splendor. Whether by day, when sunlight bathes the landscape in a golden glow, or by night, when castles are illuminated, a Rhine Gorge cruise promises unforgettable moments and panoramic vistas.

A UNESCO World Heritage Site:

The Rhine Gorge's recognition as a UNESCO World Heritage Site underscores its universal value and importance. Preservation efforts are in place to safeguard the integrity of this natural wonder, ensuring that future generations can continue to marvel at its beauty.

Enchanting Sunsets:

As the sun dips below the horizon, the Rhine Gorge transforms into a canvas of vibrant hues. Sunset cruises offer a front-row seat to this spectacular display, casting a warm glow on the castles, vineyards, and the meandering river below.

Cruise Experience:

Experiencing the Rhine Gorge from the deck of a river cruise ship is a journey through a living canvas. Whether bathed in the golden hues of sunset or surrounded by the mist of early morning, the Rhine Gorge showcases nature's artistry in every season.

Conservation Efforts and Sustainable Tourism

Embarking on a Rhine River cruise is not just a journey through picturesque landscapes and historic sites; it's an opportunity to witness and contribute to the ongoing conservation efforts and sustainable tourism initiatives that safeguard the natural beauty of this iconic waterway.

From wildlife preservation to community engagement, the Rhine prioritizes sustainability, ensuring that the allure of its shores endures for generations to come.

Balancing Tourism with Conservation:

The Rhine River, flowing through multiple countries and diverse ecosystems, recognizes the delicate balance between welcoming tourists and preserving its natural habitats.

Conservation efforts focus on minimizing the environmental impact of tourism activities, ensuring that the stunning landscapes remain unspoiled.

Wildlife Protection:

The Rhine Gorge, with its unique flora and fauna, is a haven for biodiversity. Sustainable tourism practices prioritize the protection of wildlife habitats along the riverbanks. Initiatives include the establishment of nature reserves and wildlife corridors, allowing native species to thrive in their natural environment.

Sustainable Cruising Practices:

River cruise operators along the Rhine play a crucial role in sustainable tourism. Modern cruise ships are designed with eco-friendly technologies to minimize fuel consumption and reduce emissions.

Additionally, waste management and recycling programs are implemented to ensure responsible disposal of cruise-related waste.

Shoreline Restoration Projects:

Recognizing the importance of maintaining the integrity of the Rhine's shoreline, restoration projects are underway to combat erosion and enhance natural habitats.

Planting native vegetation along the riverbanks not only stabilizes the soil but also contributes to the overall health of the ecosystem.

Community Engagement and Empowerment:

Sustainable tourism is inherently linked to the well-being of local communities along the Rhine. Initiatives that empower residents, provide economic opportunities, and involve communities in decision-making processes contribute to the long-term success of conservation efforts.

By engaging with local businesses and artisans, tourists become active contributors to the region's prosperity.

Educational Programs for Tourists:

Awareness and education are cornerstones of sustainable tourism. Cruise operators offer educational programs and guided tours that highlight the importance of conservation.

Tourists gain insights into the Rhine's ecology, its role in supporting diverse ecosystems, and the significance of responsible tourism practices.

Responsible Shore Excursions:

Shore excursions are curated to ensure they align with sustainable tourism principles. Visitors have the chance to explore local communities, cultural landmarks, and natural wonders responsibly. Guided tours emphasize the importance of minimizing disturbances to wildlife and respecting the pristine environments they encounter.

Partnerships with Conservation Organizations:

Collaborations between cruise operators, local governments, and conservation organizations strengthen the region's commitment to sustainability.

Joint initiatives focus on research, monitoring, and the implementation of best practices to safeguard the Rhine's ecosystems.

Eco-Friendly Infrastructure:

Infrastructure developments along the Rhine prioritize eco-friendly solutions. Sustainable practices in construction, such as the use of environmentally friendly materials and energy-efficient technologies, contribute to reducing the overall ecological footprint of tourism-related developments.

Future-Focused Conservation Strategies:

The commitment to conservation along the Rhine extends into the future. Continuous research, adaptive management strategies, and ongoing dialogue with stakeholders ensure that conservation efforts evolve to meet the challenges posed by a changing environment and increasing tourism.

Seasonal Highlights in Wildlife

The Rhine River and its surrounding landscapes are teeming with diverse wildlife, offering nature enthusiasts a front-row seat to the wonders of the animal kingdom.

Across the changing seasons, different species take center stage, showcasing their unique behaviors and characteristics. Here are the seasonal highlights in wildlife along the Rhine:

Spring: Awakening and Nesting

As spring breathes life back into the region, the wildlife along the Rhine undergoes a transformation. Birds, in particular, become the stars of the show. Migratory species return, filling the air with their melodic calls.

Swallows, swifts, and warblers engage in intricate aerial displays, while waterfowl like ducks and geese prepare their nests along the riverbanks. Spring is a time of renewal, and the Rhine becomes a bustling hub of avian activity.

Summer: Bustling Riverbanks

With the arrival of summer, the Rhine's wildlife reaches its peak activity. Dragonflies dance above the water, and butterflies flit among blooming wildflowers. Along the riverbanks, frogs croak, and turtles bask in the sun.

This season provides optimal conditions for observing amphibians and reptiles in their natural habitats. Additionally, summer is when many bird species raise their chicks, offering opportunities to witness adorable fledglings under the watchful eyes of their parents.

Autumn: Migration Spectacle

As temperatures begin to cool, autumn heralds one of nature's most impressive spectacles – bird migration. Raptors, such as buzzards and kestrels, take to the skies in large numbers, riding thermal currents southward.

Waterfowl gather in preparation for their long journeys, creating mesmerizing formations over the Rhine. Autumn is a prime time for birdwatchers, providing a front-row seat to this awe-inspiring migration phenomenon.

Winter: Tranquility and Waterfowl

While winter may bring a quieter ambiance to the Rhine, it offers a unique charm for wildlife enthusiasts. Waterfowl, including swans, ducks, and herons, continue to grace the river with their presence.

The bare branches along the riverbanks provide unobstructed views, making winter an excellent time for observing the subtle nuances of avian behavior. Patient observers may also spot elusive species such as kingfishers and wintering birds of prey.

Throughout the Year: Rhine's Resident Wildlife

Beyond the seasonal highlights, the Rhine is home to a variety of resident wildlife that can be observed year-round. Fish such as perch, pike, and eel inhabit the river, attracting otters and kingfishers.

European beavers, known for their dam-building prowess, contribute to the riverine ecosystem. Along the vineyard-covered slopes, butterflies and bees play a crucial role in pollination.

Conservation Efforts: Protecting Rhine's Biodiversity

Efforts are underway to protect the rich biodiversity along the Rhine. Conservation initiatives focus on preserving natural habitats, ensuring sustainable fishing practices, and maintaining water quality.

Travelers can contribute to these efforts by respecting wildlife habitats, adhering to designated paths, and supporting environmentally conscious tourism practices.

Chapter Seven
CULTURAL IMMERSION
LOCAL CUSTOMS AND TRADITIONS

Embarking on a Rhine River cruise is not just a scenic journey through breathtaking landscapes; it's also an immersive experience into the rich tapestry of local customs and traditions that have shaped the communities along the riverbanks for centuries.

Medieval Festivals: Stepping Back in Time

One of the most captivating ways to immerse yourself in the cultural history of the Rhine is by attending medieval festivals held in charming riverside towns. These events transport visitors to bygone eras, complete with period costumes, jousting tournaments, and traditional music.

Participate in lively processions and indulge in the vibrant atmosphere as locals showcase the customs that have been passed down through generations.

Wine Culture: Tasting Traditions Along the Vineyards

The terraced vineyards that grace the slopes along the Rhine are not only a testament to the region's viticultural excellence but also a living expression of its wine culture. Engage in wine tastings hosted by knowledgeable vintners who share insights into the art of winemaking.

Learn about the distinct varieties cultivated in each region, savor local vintages, and discover the age-old traditions that contribute to the production of some of Europe's finest wines.

Folklore and Rhine Legends: Tales of Lore and Mystery

The Rhine River is steeped in folklore, with legends that have been passed down through generations. Cruise past iconic castles, and you might hear tales of mythical creatures, heroic deeds, and tragic romances.

Local guides often regale passengers with captivating stories, adding a layer of enchantment to the landscapes. Explore the lore behind famous landmarks like the Lorelei Rock and delve into the mysteries that have inspired poets and storytellers for centuries.

Culinary Traditions: A Feast for the Senses

Sampling the local cuisine is an integral part of cultural immersion along the Rhine. Each region boasts its own culinary traditions, from hearty German specialties to French delicacies. Indulge in the flavors of freshly caught fish from the river, artisanal cheeses, and delectable pastries.

Engage in culinary workshops to learn the art of crafting regional dishes, and perhaps even bring home a newfound skill to share with friends and family.

Traditional Arts and Crafts: Handcrafted Heritage

Riverside towns along the Rhine are often hubs of artistic expression, showcasing traditional crafts that have endured through time. Stroll through local markets where artisans display handmade pottery, intricate woodwork, and exquisite textiles.

Engage with craftspeople, witnessing their skillful techniques and gaining insight into the cultural significance of their creations. Purchasing these unique handmade souvenirs allows travelers to take a piece of Rhine culture home with them.

Festivals and Celebrations: Shared Joy and Community

Participating in local festivals and celebrations provides a glimpse into the vibrant communal life along the Rhine. Whether it's a lively carnival, a traditional harvest festival, or a colorful parade, these events reflect the spirit and unity of the communities.

Joining in the festivities allows travelers to experience the warmth of local hospitality and witness firsthand the joyous traditions that bind people together.

Conservation and Stewardship: Preserving Cultural Heritage

In addition to celebrating age-old traditions, the Rhine River communities are actively involved in preserving their cultural heritage. Conservation efforts focus on maintaining historic structures, supporting local artisans, and fostering sustainable tourism practices.

Travelers can contribute to these initiatives by respecting cultural sites, engaging responsibly with local communities, and supporting businesses that prioritize heritage conservation.

GREETINGS AND POLITENESS

Navigating the Rhine River isn't just a journey through stunning landscapes; it's a cultural experience that involves engaging with the local communities along the way. Understanding the greetings and politeness customs of the region adds an extra layer of connection to your Rhine River cruise.

Greeting Locals: A Warm Welcome

The people along the Rhine are known for their hospitality, and a friendly greeting is the perfect way to initiate a positive interaction.

When meeting locals, a simple "Guten Tag" (Good day) in Germany, or "Bonjour" (Good morning) in France sets a welcoming tone. It's common to accompany your greeting with a smile, establishing an amicable atmosphere.

Politeness in Conversations: Courtesy is Key

Politeness is highly valued along the Rhine, and conversations often reflect this cultural norm. Use formal titles and last names when addressing individuals unless you're invited to use first names.

Adding polite phrases like "bitte" (please) and "danke" (thank you) to your interactions demonstrates respect and consideration.

Traditional Gestures: Non-Verbal Politeness

Non-verbal communication plays a role in politeness, and there are certain gestures that convey respect.

A firm handshake is a common greeting in Germany, while the French may opt for a light kiss on both cheeks. Maintaining eye contact during conversations is a sign of attentiveness and sincerity.

Dining Etiquette: Savoring the Experience

Sharing meals is a significant aspect of Rhine culture, and observing dining etiquette is a gesture of respect. Keep your hands on the table but avoid resting your elbows there, a practice considered impolite.

When toasting, maintain eye contact and say "Prost" in Germany or "Santé" in France. It's customary to wait for the host to begin the meal before you start eating.

Respecting Personal Space: Mindful Interaction

Respecting personal space is crucial in Rhine River communities. Germans, in particular, appreciate a degree of personal space during conversations.

When interacting with others, be mindful of their comfort zones, and avoid standing too close. Politeness is also extended to public spaces, where maintaining order and adhering to rules contribute to a harmonious environment.

Acknowledging Cultural Diversity: Embracing Differences

The Rhine River passes through multiple countries, each with its own cultural nuances. Embrace the diversity you encounter, and be open to learning about different customs.

If uncertain about a specific tradition, don't hesitate to ask locals for guidance. Most people appreciate visitors who show genuine interest in their culture.

Saying Goodbye: Departing with Gratitude

As your Rhine River journey concludes, saying goodbye with gratitude is a final act of politeness. Express appreciation for the warm welcome, the shared experiences, and the insights gained.

A simple "Auf Wiedersehen" (Goodbye) in Germany or "Au revoir" (Until we meet again) in France, coupled with a sincere smile, leaves a positive impression.

In essence, greetings and politeness along the Rhine are about fostering positive connections with the communities you encounter. By incorporating these cultural practices into your interactions, you not only show respect for local customs but also enrich your overall Rhine River experience.

Festivals and Celebrations

Embarking on a Rhine River cruise not only unveils breathtaking landscapes but also presents the opportunity to immerse yourself in the vibrant tapestry of local festivals and celebrations. As the river winds its way through Germany and France, each region along its banks brings its unique traditions and festivities to life.

Cologne Carnival (Kölner Karneval) - Cologne, Germany

If your Rhine River journey aligns with late winter or early spring, you might find yourself amidst the lively and colorful Cologne Carnival.

This festive extravaganza kicks off in November but reaches its peak in February, with elaborate parades, vibrant costumes, and exuberant street celebrations. Join the locals in cheering "Kölle Alaaf!" and savor the jovial atmosphere.

Rhine in Flames - Various Locations Along the Rhine

Experience the magic of the Rhine in Flames, a series of spectacular firework displays lighting up the night sky against the backdrop of historic castles and scenic landscapes.

This annual event takes place at different locations along the Rhine, including Bonn, Rüdesheim, and Oberwesel. Cruising during these events offers a front-row seat to this mesmerizing display of light and color.

Wine Festivals - Rüdesheim, Germany

The Rhine is synonymous with wine, and Rüdesheim, situated in the heart of the Rhine wine region, hosts vibrant wine festivals throughout the year.

From the Rüdesheim Wine Festival to the Assmannshausen Red Wine Festival, these events showcase the finest local wines. Sip on

Riesling or Pinot Noir while enjoying live music and the convivial ambiance of the wine culture.

Strasbourg Christmas Market - Strasbourg, France

If your Rhine River cruise aligns with the holiday season, don't miss the enchanting Strasbourg Christmas Market. Strasbourg is known as the "Capital of Christmas," and its market, dating back to 1570, is one of the oldest in Europe.

Stroll through the festively decorated streets, savor seasonal treats, and explore the market's themed villages, creating a magical atmosphere.

Koblenz Summer Festival - Koblenz, Germany

Celebrate summer along the Rhine at the Koblenz Summer Festival. This event transforms the city into a hub of music, art, and cultural performances.

Enjoy open-air concerts, art exhibitions, and culinary delights as you soak in the lively atmosphere along the riverbanks. The festival typically takes place in July, offering a perfect blend of entertainment and warm weather.

Rhine Music Festival - Various Locations

For music enthusiasts, the Rhine Music Festival is a highlight. Experience classical music performances at iconic venues along the river, including castles and historic churches. The festival attracts renowned musicians, providing a cultural feast for those with a passion for symphonies and melodies.

Rüdesheim Winegrowers' Parade - Rüdesheim, Germany

Immerse yourself in the rich winemaking tradition of the Rhine by attending the Rüdesheim Winegrowers' Parade.

This lively procession features elaborately decorated floats, traditional costumes, and local winemakers showcasing their pride. The parade, usually held in August, is a visual feast that captures the essence of the region's viticulture.

Medieval Market - Bacharach, Germany

Step back in time at the Medieval Market in Bacharach. This annual event, held in the charming medieval town, transports visitors to the days of knights, jesters, and craftsmen.

Wander through the market stalls offering handmade goods, witness historical reenactments, and enjoy the festive spirit of this unique celebration.

Wine Culture

Embarking on a Rhine River cruise is not just a scenic journey; it's an immersive experience into the rich wine culture that has flourished along the riverbanks for centuries.

As you meander through picturesque vineyards and historic wine-producing regions, the Rhine unveils a captivating tale of terroir, grape varieties, and time-honored winemaking traditions.

Rüdesheim: A Vinicultural Gem

Location: Rüdesheim, Germany

Rüdesheim stands as a vinicultural gem along the Rhine, where the steep slopes of the vineyards embrace the river, creating an ideal microclimate for grape cultivation.

This charming town, part of the Rheingau wine region, is renowned for its Riesling wines, characterized by their crisp acidity and distinctive flavors.

Highlights:

Wine Tasting Tours:

Embark on guided wine tasting tours that lead you through centuries-old cellars, where expert vintners share the nuances of Rüdesheim's prized Rieslings.

Winemaking Museums:

Explore winemaking museums, such as the Rheingau Wine Museum, offering insights into the history of winemaking in the region.

Drosselgasse:

Wander through the lively Drosselgasse, a narrow cobblestone alley lined with wine taverns and lively pubs, creating a festive atmosphere.

Mosel Valley: Home to Elegant Rieslings

Location: Mosel Valley, Germany

The Mosel Valley, a tributary of the Rhine, is celebrated for producing some of the world's most elegant and refined Rieslings. The steep slopes of the vineyards, overlooking the winding Mosel River, contribute to the unique character of the wines produced in this region.

Highlights:

Scenic Vineyard Cruises:

Take a leisurely cruise through the Mosel Valley, allowing you to appreciate the breathtaking vineyard landscapes while enjoying tastings of local Rieslings.

Reichsburg Cochem:

Visit the Reichsburg Cochem, a fairytale-like castle overlooking the Mosel, and discover its vineyards that produce exceptional wines.

Alsace: A Symphony of Aromas

Location: Alsace, France

As the Rhine winds its way through the Alsace region of France, you encounter a harmonious blend of French and German influences in winemaking. Alsace is particularly known for its aromatic white wines, including Gewürztraminer and Pinot Gris.

Highlights:

Wine Routes:

Navigate the Alsace Wine Route, a picturesque journey through vine-covered hills dotted with charming villages, where family-owned wineries invite you to savor their unique creations.

Cellar Visits:

Delve into ancient cellars, where winemakers guide you through the art of producing Alsace's renowned varietals.

Wine Tasting on Board: Savoring the Rhine's Bounty

Your Rhine River cruise itself becomes a platform for indulging in the region's wine culture. Onboard tastings feature selections from local vineyards, allowing you to sample the diverse flavors of the Rhine's wine regions without leaving the comfort of your cruise ship.

Dining Etiquette

Seating Protocol:

In the elegant dining spaces aboard your cruise ship, seating arrangements often follow an open-seating concept. However, for special dinners or themed evenings, you may find assigned seating.

Embrace the opportunity to mingle with fellow travelers, fostering a convivial atmosphere.

Formal vs. Casual Attire:

Most Rhine River cruises maintain a relaxed dress code, especially during daytime excursions and casual dinners.

However, for formal evenings or specialty dining experiences, consider dressing up a bit. This might involve cocktail attire or smart-casual wear to complement the refined ambiance.

Navigating Culinary Diversity:

The Rhine's culinary landscape is a mosaic of flavors, reflecting the cultures along its course. When faced with a menu featuring regional specialties, embrace the chance to explore new tastes.

From hearty German sausages to delicate French pastries, each dish tells a story of local traditions.

Wine Pairing Perfection:

Given the rich vinicultural heritage of the Rhine, wine often takes center stage during meals. Familiarize yourself with local wines, particularly Rieslings from the German regions, and don't hesitate to seek recommendations from onboard sommeliers for the perfect wine pairing with your chosen dish.

Multicultural Toasts:

As you engage in toasts during onboard dinners or local excursions, respect the diverse languages and customs of the regions you're traversing.

Learn a few basic phrases like "Prost!" in German or "Santé!" in French to enhance your interactions and show appreciation for the local culture.

Tipping Customs:

Tipping practices can vary across Rhine River cruise lines. Generally, gratuities may be included in the overall fare or left to the discretion of passengers.

Be aware of the cruise line's policies, and if additional tipping is customary, express your appreciation to the ship's staff for their service.

Savoring Leisurely Meals:

One of the joys of a Rhine River cruise is the unhurried pace of dining. Embrace the European tradition of lingering over meals, savoring each course.

Engage in leisurely conversations with fellow travelers, and let the ambiance of the ship's dining venues enhance your culinary experience.

Special Dietary Requests:

If you have dietary restrictions or preferences, inform the cruise staff in advance. Most Rhine River cruise lines are accommodating and can tailor meals to meet specific dietary needs, ensuring that every guest enjoys a delightful dining experience.

Local Culinary Excursions:

During onshore excursions, seize the chance to indulge in local culinary delights. Participate in guided food tours, visit bustling markets, and relish authentic dishes prepared by skilled local chefs. This immersive approach allows you to connect with the culinary soul of each destination.

Expressing Appreciation:

Show your gratitude for exceptional service by expressing your appreciation to the culinary and service teams. A sincere thank you and positive feedback go a long way in creating a warm and memorable dining experience for everyone on board.

Religious Customs

As you embark on a Rhine River cruise, you'll encounter a rich tapestry of religious customs woven into the cultural fabric of the regions along its banks.

From Gothic cathedrals to serene chapels nestled in vineyard-covered hills, the Rhine's landscapes are adorned with symbols of spiritual devotion. Here's a glimpse into the religious customs that add a layer of sacred beauty to your journey:

Gothic Grandeur: Cologne Cathedral (Cologne, Germany):

Your Rhine River cruise may commence in the shadow of one of Europe's most iconic cathedrals, Cologne Cathedral. This masterpiece of Gothic architecture, dedicated to St. Peter and St. Mary, stands as a testament to the enduring spirit of faith.

Religious Significance:

Cologne Cathedral is a significant pilgrimage site housing the Shrine of the Three Kings, believed to hold relics of the Biblical Magi. Pilgrims and visitors alike are drawn to the awe-inspiring interiors adorned with stained glass windows, intricate sculptures, and a profound sense of spiritual reverence.

Spiritual Oasis: Strasbourg- Grande île (Strasbourg, France):

The charming city of Strasbourg, nestled along the Rhine, boasts a UNESCO-listed historic center on Grande île. Amid its cobblestone streets and half-timbered houses, you'll find St. Thomas Church, a tranquil oasis of spiritual reflection.

Religious Significance:

St. Thomas Church is renowned for its elegant architecture and historical significance. It served as a place of worship for figures like Johannes Gutenberg and Albert Schweitzer.

Take a moment to appreciate the serenity within its walls, reflecting the harmonious coexistence of faith and culture.

Historical Reverence: Speyer Cathedral (Speyer, Germany):

Speyer Cathedral, a UNESCO World Heritage site, stands as a magnificent example of Romanesque architecture. Its imposing structure and serene surroundings make it a compelling stop along the Rhine.

Religious Significance:

Speyer Cathedral holds the tombs of German emperors, including Rudolf I and Conrad II. The cathedral's enduring presence speaks to the intertwining of religious and historical narratives, inviting contemplation on the passage of time and the resilience of faith.

Island of Worship: Mainau (Lake Constance, Germany):

While not directly on the Rhine, the island of Mainau in Lake Constance offers a unique spiritual experience. Known as the "Island of Flowers," Mainau hosts the Chapel of St. Mary, surrounded by vibrant gardens and stunning lake views.

Religious Significance:

The Chapel of St. Mary provides a tranquil space for reflection amidst nature's beauty. Whether you attend a service or simply appreciate the serenity of the chapel's surroundings, Mainau offers a harmonious blend of natural and spiritual wonders.

Riverside Reflection: Rüdesheim am Rhein: Wine and Pilgrimage (Rüdesheim, Germany):

Rüdesheim, a charming town nestled in the vineyards of the Rhine Valley, holds not only oenophilic delights but also a spiritual gem—Klunkhardshof Chapel.

Religious Significance:

Klunkhardshof Chapel, also known as the Winegrowers' Chapel, is a testament to the deep connection between winemaking traditions and spirituality. Pilgrims and locals alike visit this intimate chapel, reflecting on the intertwining threads of faith and the cultural heritage of winemaking.

Interfaith Harmony: Marksburg Castle (Braubach, Germany):

While not a place of worship, Marksburg Castle stands as a symbol of interfaith harmony. This medieval fortress on the banks of the Rhine represents the coexistence of diverse religious and cultural influences.

As you explore Marksburg Castle, appreciate the historical context of a region where various faiths have shaped the landscape. The castle's survival through centuries echoes the resilience of shared history and the enduring spirit of the people.

Expressions of Faith: Rhine Gorge (Germany):

Cruising through the picturesque Rhine Gorge, you'll encounter numerous small chapels and wayside shrines along the riverbanks. These unassuming structures silently testify to the enduring faith of local communities.

Each chapel and shrine serves as a quiet space for contemplation and prayer. Whether perched on a hilltop or nestled in a vineyard, these expressions of faith add a spiritual dimension to the breathtaking landscapes of the Rhine Gorge.

Cultural Festivals and Religious Celebrations:

Throughout your Rhine River cruise, you may have the opportunity to witness cultural festivals and religious celebrations that reflect the diversity of traditions along the river.

These events provide insight into the communal expressions of faith and the vibrant tapestry of religious customs.

Religious Significance:

Participating in or observing local festivals allows you to connect with the spiritual heartbeat of the communities you encounter.

Whether it's a medieval religious procession, a lively street festival, or a traditional ceremony, these moments offer a glimpse into the profound cultural and spiritual heritage of the Rhine's inhabitants.

Folklore and Superstitions

The Lore of Lorelei:

As the sun sets over the Rhine Gorge, the legend of Lorelei comes to life. This iconic rock formation near St. Goarshausen is said to be the dwelling place of a siren, Lorelei, whose mesmerizing song lured sailors to their demise.

Significance:

Folklore warns of the irresistible allure of Lorelei's song, a symbol of the river's mysterious and sometimes treacherous nature. Embrace the enchantment of Lorelei's legend as you cruise past this dramatic landscape, where myth and reality intertwine.

The Nix and Nixe:

Folklore introduces you to the Nix and Nixe, water spirits believed to inhabit the Rhine's depths. These mystical beings are said to possess the ability to shape-shift and often appear as alluring figures, tempting those who venture too close to the water's edge.

Significance:

The tales of Nix and Nixe serve as cautionary narratives, reminding travelers to respect the unpredictable currents of the Rhine. Keep an eye out for these mythical beings as you navigate the river's twists and turns, acknowledging the mystique that lies beneath its surface.

The Guardian of Boppard: The Bopparder Hamm Lion:

Boppard is home to the Bopparder Hamm Lion, a legendary guardian said to protect the town from harm. This lion statue, perched high above the Rhine, is believed to possess mystical powers.

Significance:

According to local superstitions, the Bopparder Hamm Lion safeguards the town and its inhabitants. As you pass Boppard, appreciate the symbolism of this mythical guardian, standing as a testament to the enduring belief in protective spirits along the Rhine.

The Healing Waters of St. Rochus Spring:

At St. Goarshausen, discover the St. Rochus Spring, renowned for its healing properties. Legend has it that the water from this spring has the power to cure various ailments.

Significance:

Locals and visitors alike have embraced the belief in the therapeutic qualities of St. Rochus Spring. Engage with this centuries-old tradition by experiencing the waters for yourself, allowing the mysticism of the healing spring to become part of your Rhine adventure.

The Wishing Well of Rüdesheim:

Rüdesheim is home to a charming wishing well known as the Brömserhof Brunnen. Visitors are invited to make a wish and drop a coin into the well, believing that their wishes will come true.

Significance:

Engage in this delightful tradition and toss a coin into the Brömserhof Brunnen, embracing the folklore that surrounds the power of wishes along the Rhine. Allow the whimsical spirit of the well to add a touch of magic to your journey.

The Magical Atmosphere of Christmas Markets:

If your Rhine River cruise coincides with the winter season, immerse yourself in the enchanting atmosphere of Christmas markets along the riverbanks. These markets are steeped in festive traditions and folklore, creating a magical ambiance.

Significance:

Embrace the warmth of seasonal folklore as you explore the Christmas markets. From tales of holiday spirits to the magic of twinkling lights, the festive folklore of the Rhine comes alive during this special time of year.

Riverbank Tales: Local Legends and Anecdotes:

Each charming village and town along the Rhine has its own collection of local legends and anecdotes. From heroic tales to humorous anecdotes, these stories contribute to the cultural richness of the region.

Significance:

Engage with locals and guides who may share these captivating tales, offering insights into the folklore that has shaped Rhine communities. Allow these stories to paint a vivid picture of the Rhine's cultural landscape.

Arts and Crafts

From traditional craftsmanship to contemporary expressions, the Rhine's banks are adorned with creativity that adds a unique flair to your journey.

The Artistry of Rhine Vineyards:

Rhine vineyards are not only sources of exquisite wines but also canvases for artistic expression. The meticulously arranged vine rows, forming patterns across the hillsides, showcase the artistry of viticulture.

Take in the visual poetry of vineyard landscapes, where the art of winemaking merges seamlessly with the natural beauty of the Rhine Valley. From the orderly lines of grapevines to the changing colors with the seasons, witness the artistry of agriculture along the riverbanks.

The Craft of Rhine Wine Labels:

Wine labels along the Rhine are not merely informative; they are works of art. Many wineries collaborate with local artists to create labels that reflect the essence of the wine and the region.

Appreciate the attention to detail and creativity that goes into designing wine labels. The labels serve as visual storytellers, providing a glimpse into the character and heritage of each bottle. Explore local wineries to discover the diverse artistic interpretations adorning Rhine wines.

Historic Art in Cathedrals and Churches:

Cathedrals and churches along the Rhine are veritable galleries of historical art. From stained glass windows to intricately carved altars, these sacred spaces are adorned with masterpieces that span centuries.

Immerse yourself in the artistry of religious architecture as you explore cathedrals like Cologne Cathedral and churches in towns along the Rhine.

The craftsmanship and symbolism within these structures offer a visual journey through the region's cultural and religious history.

Rhine-inspired Painting and Photography:

The scenic beauty of the Rhine serves as a muse for many artists. Painters and photographers capture the river's landscapes, castles, and charming villages, creating works that celebrate the visual allure of the region.

Explore local art galleries and studios that feature Rhine-inspired artwork. Whether it's a canvas capturing the play of sunlight on the river or a photograph showcasing the timeless beauty of a medieval town, these artistic expressions offer a fresh perspective on the Rhine's aesthetics.

Handcrafted Souvenirs at Local Markets:

Local markets along the Rhine are treasure troves of handcrafted souvenirs. From ceramics and textiles to jewelry and woodwork, artisans showcase their talents, offering visitors a chance to take home a piece of the region's craftsmanship.

Stroll through markets like those in Rüdesheim or Strasbourg, where you'll encounter artisans displaying their creations.

Support local craftsmanship by choosing unique souvenirs that reflect the artistic diversity of the Rhine's communities.

Contemporary Art Installations:

Some Rhine towns embrace contemporary art, featuring installations and exhibits that add a modern twist to their cultural landscapes. Public spaces may host sculptures, murals, or interactive artworks, creating a dynamic visual experience.

Keep an eye out for contemporary art installations as you explore towns like Basel or Düsseldorf. These pieces offer a juxtaposition of the historic surroundings with contemporary creativity, showcasing the evolving cultural scene along the Rhine.

Artisan Workshops and Demonstrations:

Delve into the world of craftsmanship through artisan workshops and demonstrations. Some towns host events where skilled artisans showcase their techniques, providing insights into traditional methods of creating pottery, glassware, or textiles.

Participate in or observe these workshops to gain a deeper appreciation for the labor-intensive processes behind handmade crafts. Engaging with artisans allows you to connect with the living traditions of the Rhine's artistic heritage.

CULINARY DELIGHTS OF THE RHINE

Cologne's Culinary Palette

Cologne, located along the scenic Rhine River, boasts a culinary palette as diverse and rich as its history. From traditional German delights to innovative international cuisine, the city's food scene invites visitors on a gastronomic journey.

Start your culinary exploration in Cologne with a taste of the iconic local dish, Kölsche Hänchen. This roasted chicken, marinated in a secret blend of spices, captures the essence of Cologne's culinary traditions. Pair it with a glass of Kölsch, the city's distinctive beer, served in small glasses to ensure freshness.

Venture into Cologne's historic Old Town, where the fragrance of freshly baked bread leads you to the quaint bakeries that line the cobblestone streets. Savor the rustic goodness of traditional German bread, pretzels, and pastries, each revealing the craftsmanship that has been perfected over generations.

For a more refined dining experience, explore Cologne's modern gastronomic landscape. The city has embraced international influences, and innovative chefs are creating a fusion of flavors that tantalize the taste buds. At Michelin-starred restaurants like Hanse Stube, indulge in a culinary journey where precision and creativity converge on the plate.

Cologne's food markets are a treasure trove for food enthusiasts. The Cologne Cathedral backdrop provides a stunning setting for the Cologne Cathedral Christmas Market, where local vendors showcase an array of festive treats. Sample artisanal chocolates, gingerbread cookies, and mulled wine as you immerse yourself in the holiday spirit.

Delve into the Rhine's bounty by trying the freshwater delights at one of Cologne's seafood restaurants. From succulent river fish to delectable shrimp, these establishments celebrate the river's offerings, providing a fresh and unique dining experience.

Vegetarian and vegan options have found their place in Cologne's culinary repertoire. Explore trendy cafes and restaurants that prioritize sustainability and organic ingredients, offering plant-based dishes that are both flavorful and innovative.

The city's multicultural vibe is evident in its diverse food offerings. International cuisines, ranging from Italian to Vietnamese, are well-represented, reflecting Cologne's cosmopolitan nature. Embark on a culinary adventure through the Belgian Quarter, where hip eateries serve up global flavors in a trendy setting.

Don't miss out on the local street food scene. Wander through outdoor markets and festivals to discover stalls offering bratwurst, currywurst, and other beloved German street foods. These quick bites are not just delicious; they also provide a glimpse into the lively street culture of Cologne.

Cap off your culinary journey with a visit to a traditional brewery, where the art of beer brewing is celebrated. Engage in the convivial atmosphere of a beer garden or historic pub, where locals and tourists alike come together to enjoy the city's liquid gold.

Local Delicacies in Amsterdam

Amsterdam, a city known for its picturesque canals and vibrant culture, also offers a delightful array of local delicacies that reflect its rich culinary heritage. Dive into the unique flavors of Amsterdam with these tempting treats.

Begin your culinary journey with Amsterdam's iconic stroopwafels. These thin waffle cookies are filled with a gooey caramel syrup.

The combination of the crispy exterior and the sweet, sticky interior makes them an irresistible treat. Try them fresh from local markets or dedicated stroopwafel shops.

Bitterballen:

A quintessential Dutch snack, bitterballen are deep-fried balls filled with a creamy mixture of beef or veal ragout. Typically served with mustard, these savory delights are a popular choice at pubs and social gatherings.

Haring:

For seafood enthusiasts, haring is a must-try. This raw herring fish is often served with onions and pickles. Embrace the local tradition by holding the fish by its tail and taking a bite – a unique and authentic Amsterdam experience.

Dutch Cheese:

Amsterdam's markets are a haven for cheese lovers. Sample a variety of Dutch cheeses, including Gouda and Edam, each with its own distinct flavor profile. Pair them with fresh bread or fruits for a delightful tasting experience.

Poffertjes:

Satisfy your sweet tooth with poffertjes, small fluffy pancakes dusted with powdered sugar. Often served with a dollop of butter, these bite-sized delights are a beloved Dutch treat found at street markets and pancake houses.

Dutch Fries with Diverse Sauces:

Indulge in a cone of Dutch fries, thicker than traditional fries, and explore an array of sauces. From classic mayonnaise to unique toppings like peanut sauce or ketchup with onions, the Dutch take their fries seriously, offering a flavor for every palate.

Erwtensoep (Pea Soup):

Especially popular during the colder months, erwtensoep is a hearty split pea soup with chunks of pork or sausage. This comforting dish is a local favorite, often enjoyed with rye bread and bacon.

Dutch Apple Pie:

Cap off your Amsterdam culinary adventure with a slice of Dutch apple pie. Laden with spiced apples and encased in a buttery crust, this dessert is a sweet conclusion to your exploration of local flavors.

Amsterdam's diverse and flavorful culinary scene showcases a mix of traditional and modern delights. Whether you're strolling through markets, visiting local eateries, or enjoying the city's charming cafes, these local delicacies promise a gastronomic journey that mirrors the cultural richness of Amsterdam.

Romantic Rhine: Vineyards and Gastronomy

The Romantic Rhine, adorned with picturesque vineyards and charming villages, beckons lovers to a romantic getaway blending scenic beauty with exquisite gastronomy. Here's a glimpse into the enchanting world of Rhine's vineyards and the delectable culinary experiences that await.

Vineyard Romance:

Embark on a romantic journey through the Rhine Valley's vine-covered landscapes. The terraced vineyards along the riverbanks produce some of the finest wines in the world.

Visit renowned wineries in regions like the Middle Rhine or Rheingau to savor the nuances of Riesling, the signature grape of the area. Take a leisurely stroll through the vineyards, hand in hand, as you admire the rows of vines overlooking the serene river.

Wine Tasting Extravaganza:

Immerse yourselves in the art of wine tasting at historic cellars and modern estates. Engage with knowledgeable vintners who share the stories behind each vintage. From crisp and refreshing whites to robust reds, the Rhine Valley's diverse wine selection caters to every palate.

Indulge in a private tasting session, allowing the rich flavors to deepen your connection amid the romantic ambiance of the vineyards.

Gourmet Delights Along the Rhine:

Rhine's gastronomic scene complements its wine culture, offering an array of culinary delights to elevate your romantic escapade. In charming riverside towns, explore local restaurants that showcase the region's culinary expertise.

Enjoy a candlelit dinner with panoramic views of the Rhine, savoring dishes crafted from fresh, locally sourced ingredients.

Regional Specialties:

Delight your taste buds with regional specialties that pair seamlessly with the local wines. Try Flammkuchen, a thin-crust pizza topped with crème fraîche, onions, and bacon, offering a perfect blend of textures and flavors. Sample the local river fish, like trout or perch, prepared with finesse at waterside eateries.

Rhine River Cruises:

Enhance your romantic experience with a leisurely Rhine River cruise. Glide along the water, relishing the scenic beauty of vineyard-clad hillsides. Some cruises offer onboard wine tastings, allowing you to savor local vintages while drifting through the heart of wine country.

Wine Festivals and Events:

Plan your visit around one of the Rhine's vibrant wine festivals or events. Join locals in celebrating the grape harvest or attend wine tastings hosted in charming squares. These lively gatherings infuse the air with merriment, creating an unforgettable backdrop for your romantic interlude.

Strasbourg's Fusion of French and German Influences

Strasbourg, nestled at the crossroads of France and Germany, boasts a captivating fusion of cultural influences reflected not only in its architecture but also in its culinary landscape.

This harmonious blend creates a unique experience for visitors, where French finesse meets German precision in a city that exudes charm and sophistication.

Architected Elegance:

Strasbourg's architecture seamlessly marries French and German styles. The iconic Strasbourg Cathedral, a masterpiece of Gothic architecture, stands tall, while the half-timbered houses in La Petite France exude the charm of a German fairytale village. This architectural fusion mirrors the city's cultural diversity.

Culinary Tapestry:

Strasbourg's gastronomy mirrors its dual identity, offering a delectable fusion of French and German culinary traditions. Indulge in the city's renowned Alsatian cuisine, where the flavors of both nations come together.

Try Tarte Flambée, a thin-crust pizza-like dish topped with crème fraîche, onions, and bacon, or Choucroute garnie, a hearty dish featuring sauerkraut, sausages, and other meats.

Winstubs and Brasseries:

Winstubs, traditional Alsatian taverns, and French-style brasseries dot the city, offering a diverse range of culinary experiences. Enjoy a leisurely meal in these charming establishments, where you can savor local wines alongside

Alsatian and French specialties. The convivial atmosphere captures the essence of Strasbourg's cultural amalgamation.

Bilingual Ambiance:

Strasbourg's bilingual nature, with both French and German spoken interchangeably, adds to its unique character. The city's street signs, menus, and conversations reflect this linguistic diversity, creating an immersive experience for visitors eager to explore both cultural facets.

Christmas Markets Extravaganza:

During the festive season, Strasbourg's Christmas markets come alive with a magical atmosphere. The blend of French elegance and German festive traditions is evident in the market stalls offering crafts, local treats, and the enchanting decorations that transform the city into a winter wonderland.

European Union Hub:

As the seat of several European institutions, Strasbourg serves as a symbol of unity. Its role in the European Union further emphasizes its position as a cultural bridge, where French and German influences converge in a spirit of collaboration and cooperation.

River Rhine Connectivity:

The Rhine River, flowing through Strasbourg, historically connected France and Germany. Today, boat tours along the river provide a scenic journey, allowing visitors to appreciate the landscape that has shaped Strasbourg's cultural identity.

DINING ABOARD THE CRUISE SHIP

Dining aboard a cruise ship is a culinary journey that transcends the boundaries of the sea, offering a diverse and indulgent experience for passengers. From casual buffets to fine dining, cruise ship cuisine is designed to cater to a wide range of tastes and preferences.

Culinary Variety:

Cruise ships are renowned for their diverse culinary offerings. Passengers can explore a multitude of dining venues, including formal dining rooms, specialty restaurants, casual buffets, and even grab-and-go options. This variety ensures that there's something to suit every palate and dining mood.

Formal Dining Elegance:

Experience the epitome of cruise ship dining in formal dining rooms. These elegant spaces often offer multi-course meals with attentive service. Passengers can relish gourmet dishes prepared by skilled chefs, all while enjoying the sophisticated ambiance of these venues.

Specialty Restaurants:

Cruise ships frequently feature specialty restaurants that focus on specific cuisines or culinary themes. These venues provide a more intimate setting and often require reservations.

From steakhouses to seafood grills and Italian bistros, specialty restaurants elevate the dining experience with curated menus and distinctive atmospheres.

Casual Al Fresco Dining:

For a more relaxed experience, cruise ships often offer casual al fresco dining options. Passengers can enjoy their meals with ocean views, whether it's a light lunch by the pool or a sunset dinner on an open deck. This laid-back setting adds a touch of romance and relaxation to the culinary adventure.

Theme Nights and Culinary Events:

Cruise ships frequently host theme nights and culinary events. Passengers can indulge in themed buffets, such as seafood nights or international cuisine extravaganzas. These events add an element of excitement and variety to the onboard dining experience.

Room Service Convenience:

For those seeking privacy or a more intimate setting, room service is often available 24/7. Passengers can enjoy a quiet breakfast on their private balcony or a cozy dinner in the comfort of their cabin, creating a personalized dining experience at their own pace.

All-Inclusive Options:

Many cruise lines offer all-inclusive dining options, where certain specialty restaurants and dining experiences are included in the cruise fare. This allows passengers to savor a wide array of culinary delights without worrying about additional costs.

Culinary Classes and Demonstrations:

To enhance the onboard experience, cruise ships often offer culinary classes and demonstrations. Passengers can participate in cooking classes, wine tastings, and culinary workshops led by skilled chefs, adding an educational and interactive element to their journey.

Chapter Eight
ACTIVITIES AND EXCURSIONS
GUIDED TOURS AND SHORE EXCURSIONS

Exploring Cultural Gems:

Embarking on a Rhine River cruise unveils a tapestry of cultural gems, each port of call promising a rich blend of history, art, and local traditions. From medieval castles perched on hillsides to charming villages with cobblestone streets, the cultural exploration along the Rhine is a journey through time.

Guided tours and shore excursions enhance this experience, offering a brilliant insight into the cultural treasures that line the riverbanks.

Medieval Marvels:

Guided tours along the Rhine often include visits to medieval castles that stand as silent witnesses to centuries of history. The iconic Marksburg Castle, towering above the town of Braubach, invites travelers to step back in time.

Explore the fortified walls, grand halls, and captivating stories that echo through the stone corridors, providing a glimpse into the medieval life that once thrived along the Rhine.

Enchanting Villages:

Shore excursions lead to enchanting villages like Bacharach and Rüdesheim, where half-timbered houses and narrow alleys transport visitors to a bygone era. Wander through cobblestone streets lined with charming shops and taverns, and let the medieval charm of these villages captivate your imagination.

Guided walking tours provide historical context, unraveling the stories embedded in the architecture and local folklore.

Artistic Treasures:

Explore the artistic treasures of the Rhine's cultural landscape through guided visits to museums and galleries. In cities like Cologne, the Cologne Cathedral Treasury showcases religious artifacts, while the Ludwig Museum exhibits a remarkable collection of modern art.

Shore excursions offer curated experiences for art enthusiasts, allowing them to delve into the vibrant cultural scenes of Rhine-side cities.

Architectural Wonders:

Cruise passengers can marvel at architectural wonders such as the Cologne Cathedral, a masterpiece of Gothic architecture. Guided tours reveal the intricate details of this UNESCO World Heritage site, from its towering spires to the stunning stained glass windows.

Delve into the architectural evolution of cities like Strasbourg, where the blend of French and German influences is evident in structures like the Strasbourg Cathedral and Maison Kammerzell.

Wine Tasting in the Vineyards:

The cultural identity of the Rhine is intertwined with its vineyards. Guided tours take wine enthusiasts to explore the terraced slopes of the vine-covered hills.

Enjoy wine tastings at local wineries, where passionate vintners share the secrets of their craft. The Rheingau region, renowned for its Riesling, provides a sensory journey through the flavors that have defined the area for centuries.

Musical Heritage:

The Rhine resonates with a rich musical heritage, and guided tours often showcase this cultural aspect. In cities like Bonn, birthplace of Beethoven, explore the composer's home, now a museum dedicated to his life and work.

Attend classical concerts in historic venues along the Rhine, immersing yourself in the melodies that have echoed through these river valleys.

Local Festivals and Traditions:

Cruise excursions align with local festivals and traditions, providing an immersive cultural experience.

Whether it's joining the vibrant atmosphere of Strasbourg's Christmas markets or participating in the folklore festivities of a riverside town, guided tours offer a chance to witness and engage in the living cultural traditions of the Rhine.

Cultural Talks and Lectures:

Enhancing the cultural exploration, cruise lines often offer onboard cultural talks and lectures. Experts share insights into the history, art, and traditions of the regions along the Rhine, enriching the overall experience and providing context for the wonders encountered during shore excursions.

Castle Adventures:

Embarking on a castle adventure along the Rhine River unveils a realm of medieval marvels, where turreted fortresses and majestic strongholds perch atop hillsides, narrating tales of chivalry, power, and architectural prowess.

From the imposing Marksburg Castle to the romantic Burg Eltz, each castle encountered during the journey invites travelers to step into a bygone era, where knights roamed and legends were forged.

Marksburg Castle:

As the only hill castle along the Middle Rhine that has never been destroyed, Marksburg Castle stands proudly, offering an authentic glimpse into medieval life. Guided tours through its towers, chambers, and ramparts provide a fascinating journey through the castle's history.

Uncover the secrets of the medieval kitchen, admire the armory, and enjoy panoramic views of the Rhine Valley from its commanding position.

Burg Eltz:

Nestled in a dense forest, Burg Eltz is a fairytale castle that seems untouched by time. Its romantic setting and well-preserved medieval architecture make it a highlight of any castle adventure.

Guided tours through its inner courtyards and furnished rooms reveal the stories of the Eltz family, showcasing a harmonious blend of Romanesque, Gothic, Renaissance, and Baroque styles.

Heidelberg Castle:

Perched above the city of Heidelberg, the Heidelberg Castle is a striking ensemble of buildings that bear witness to centuries of history. Guided tours explore the Great Barrel, the largest wine barrel in the world, and the elegant Renaissance courtyard.

The castle's terraced gardens offer panoramic views of the Neckar River, creating a picturesque backdrop for a journey through German history.

Rhinefels Castle:

Rhinefels Castle, overlooking the town of St. Goar, is a massive fortress that played a strategic role in the Middle Ages.

Guided tours unravel the castle's military significance, exploring its labyrinthine tunnels and towers. The castle's expansive grounds and views of the Rhine River add to the allure of this formidable stronghold.

Cochem Castle:

The Reichsburg Cochem, perched high above the Moselle River, is a captivating castle with a storied past. Guided tours delve into its medieval architecture and showcase the opulent rooms, including the Knight's Hall and the Emperor's Room.

The castle's hilltop location provides breathtaking views of the surrounding vineyards and the picturesque town of Cochem.

Rheinstein Castle:

Rheinstein Castle, perched on a rocky outcrop, exudes a romantic charm that transports visitors to a bygone era.

Guided tours highlight its medieval architecture, including the knight's hall and the courtyard with its well-preserved defense mechanisms.The castle's strategic location offers panoramic views of the Rhine, creating a mesmerizing experience for castle enthusiasts.

Katz Castle:

Katz Castle, overlooking the town of St. Goarshausen, is an impressive fortress with a turbulent history. Guided tours explore its sturdy walls and towers, revealing tales of medieval conflicts and strategic importance.

The castle's location along the Rhine adds a dramatic backdrop to the exploration, making it a captivating stop for castle adventurers.

Cultural Events and Festivals:

Castle adventures along the Rhine often coincide with cultural events and festivals held within these historic walls.

From medieval reenactments to classical concerts, these events transport visitors to the times when these castles were vibrant centers of life and culture, creating an immersive and unforgettable experience.

Culinary Expeditions:

Alsatian Delicacies:

Start your culinary expedition in Alsace, where the fusion of French and German influences results in a unique gastronomic experience. Sample Alsatian specialties like Flammkuchen, a thin-crust pizza with crème fraîche, onions, and bacon.

Explore charming villages like Strasbourg and Colmar, where local eateries serve regional delights such as Choucroute garnie, a hearty dish of sauerkraut and assorted meats.

Wine Tasting in the Rheingau:

Navigate through the terraced vineyards of the Rheingau region, where the renowned Riesling grape flourishes. Participate in wine tastings at local wineries, guided by passionate vintners who share the nuances of their craft.

Savor the crisp, aromatic notes of Rhine wines while enjoying the breathtaking views of the vine-covered hills.

Cologne's Culinary Palette:

Explore the diverse culinary scene of Cologne, where traditional German dishes blend with international flavors. Indulge in Kölsche Hänchen, a marinated roasted chicken, paired with the city's distinctive Kölsch beer.

Visit the vibrant street markets and sample local street foods like bratwurst and currywurst, immersing yourself in the lively street culture of this dynamic city.

Dutch Delights in Amsterdam:

As you cruise into Amsterdam, dive into the city's culinary delights. Explore the local markets offering Dutch cheeses, stroopwafels, and haring (raw herring).

Indulge in poffertjes, small fluffy pancakes, and savor Dutch apple pie in the cozy ambiance of Amsterdam's cafes. The city's multicultural vibe is reflected in its diverse restaurant scene, offering international cuisines that cater to every taste.

Culinary Festivals and Events:

Plan your culinary expeditions around local festivals and events that celebrate the gastronomic heritage of the Rhine regions.

Whether it's joining the Cologne Cathedral Christmas Market or attending wine festivals along the Rhine, these events add a festive and immersive element to your culinary journey.

Riverfront Dining in Strasbourg:

In Strasbourg, indulge in riverfront dining along the Ill River. Enjoy Alsatian specialties in charming Winstubs or French cuisine in brasseries with panoramic views.

The blend of French and German influences is evident in Strasbourg's culinary scene, offering a diverse range of culinary delights to savor.

Gastronomic River Cruises:

Enhance your culinary expedition with themed river cruises dedicated to gastronomy. Some cruise lines offer culinary-focused itineraries with onboard cooking classes, food and wine pairings, and visits to local markets. Immerse yourself in the culinary arts as you traverse the Rhine's scenic landscapes.

Local Street Food Adventures:

Embark on local street food adventures in each port of call. From Dutch fries with diverse sauces to German pretzels and Belgian chocolates, the street food offerings along the Rhine provide a delightful journey for your taste buds.

Engage with local vendors, try regional specialties, and let the flavors of the riverbanks tantalize your senses.

Scenic Walks and Nature Escapes:

Embarking on scenic walks and nature escapes along the Rhine River unveils a picturesque landscape where lush vineyards, charming villages, and serene riverbanks create an idyllic setting for exploration.

From leisurely strolls through historic towns to invigorating hikes along vineyard-clad hills, the Rhine offers a myriad of opportunities for nature enthusiasts and those seeking a peaceful retreat.

Riverside Promenades:

Take leisurely walks along the scenic riverside promenades that grace the towns along the Rhine. In cities like Strasbourg and Cologne, riverfront paths offer stunning views of architectural landmarks and the flowing waters. Enjoy a peaceful stroll, savoring the blend of urban charm and natural beauty.

Rhine Gorge Hiking Trails:

Venture into the heart of the Rhine Gorge, a UNESCO World Heritage site, where the river winds through steep vineyard-covered hills.

Hiking trails along the ridges provide breathtaking panoramas of the meandering river and the medieval castles that dot the landscape. These trails offer both serene nature escapes and opportunities for immersive historical exploration.

Vineyard Walks in Rheingau:

Embark on scenic walks through the terraced vineyards of the Rheingau region. Wander along the rows of vines, absorbing the tranquility of the landscape and enjoying the fresh air.

Many vineyards welcome visitors to explore their grounds, offering a sensory experience amid the lush greenery and the aroma of ripening grapes.

Stroll through La Petite France:

In Strasbourg, stroll through the enchanting neighborhood of La Petite France. Cobblestone streets, timber-framed houses, and flower-filled balconies create a fairy-tale ambiance.

Take a leisurely walk along the canals, enjoying the reflection of historic buildings in the water, and immerse yourself in the timeless charm of this picturesque district.

Cozy Villages Along the Moselle:

Explore the cozy villages along the Moselle River, such as Cochem and Bernkastel-Kues. These charming towns offer scenic walks through narrow alleys lined with half-timbered houses.

Meander along the riverbanks, absorb the tranquility of the surroundings, and perhaps enjoy a glass of local wine in a riverside cafe.

Hiking the Drachenfels:

For a more challenging nature escape, consider hiking the Drachenfels, a striking hill crowned by a castle ruin near Bonn.

Trails wind through lush forests, leading to panoramic viewpoints overlooking the Rhine. The ascent rewards hikers with not only breathtaking vistas but also a sense of accomplishment.

Rheinaue Park in Bonn:

Enjoy a nature escape within the city at Rheinaue Park in Bonn. This expansive park, situated along the Rhine, offers walking trails, botanical gardens, and serene lakes. It's an ideal spot for a leisurely stroll, picnics, or simply unwinding amidst nature.

Cycling Along the Rhine:

For a dynamic nature experience, consider cycling along dedicated Rhine River cycling paths. These well-maintained routes lead through picturesque landscapes, allowing you to cover more ground while enjoying the scenic beauty. Bike rentals are often available in many Rhine-side towns.

CUSTOMIZING YOUR EXPERIENCE:

Customizing your Rhine River experience allows you to tailor your journey to personal preferences, ensuring that every moment along the river reflects your interests and desires.

Whether you're drawn to cultural exploration, culinary delights, nature escapes, or a mix of everything, here are some tips to help you create a personalized Rhine adventure:

Choose Your Cruise Itinerary:

Select a cruise itinerary that aligns with your interests. Some itineraries focus more on cultural excursions, while others may emphasize scenic landscapes or culinary experiences. Consider the duration of the cruise and the ports of call to ensure they match your preferences.

Culinary Exploration:

If you're a food enthusiast, opt for cruises that offer culinary-themed experiences. Look for onboard cooking classes, wine tastings, and excursions to renowned local markets or vineyards.

Customize your dining preferences, indicating any dietary restrictions to ensure a tailored culinary experience.

Cultural Immersion:

For those seeking cultural immersion, choose guided tours and shore excursions that delve into the history, art, and traditions of each destination. Explore museums, historical sites, and attend local events or festivals. Look for themed cruises that focus on cultural enrichment.

Nature and Active Pursuits:

If nature escapes and outdoor activities appeal to you, consider itineraries that include opportunities for hiking, cycling, or simply strolling along scenic paths. Customize your excursions to include visits to nature reserves, parks, or historic landmarks surrounded by natural beauty.

Onboard Activities:

Explore the onboard activities offered by the cruise line. Whether it's themed lectures, live performances, or wellness programs, choose activities that align with your interests. Many cruise lines provide a variety of options to cater to different tastes.

Cabin Preferences:

Select a cabin category that suits your preferences. Whether you prefer a balcony for panoramic views, a suite for added luxury, or an interior cabin for a cozy retreat, your accommodation choice can enhance your overall cruise experience.

Flexible Dining Options:

Choose cruise lines that offer flexible dining options. Some ships provide open-seating dining, allowing you to dine at your preferred time. This flexibility ensures that you can align your meals with your daily activities and exploration plans.

Personalized Excursions:

Consider arranging personalized excursions or private tours at specific ports of call. This allows you to explore destinations at your own pace and focus on activities that truly interest you, providing a more intimate and customized experience.

Themed Cruises:

Explore themed cruises that cater to specific interests, such as wine cruises, art cruises, or wellness cruises. These themed experiences provide a deeper dive into your chosen passion and often include specialized activities, experts, and excursions.

Pre- and Post-Cruise Plans:

Extend your Rhine River experience by customizing pre- and post-cruise plans. Spend extra time in embarkation or disembarkation cities, exploring at your leisure and immersing yourself in the local culture.

Recommended Guided Tours And Shore Excursions Company

While specific recommendations for guided tours and shore excursions can depend on your preferences, several reputable companies are known for providing high-quality experiences along the Rhine River. Here are a few well-regarded tour operators that offer guided tours and shore excursions:

Viking River Cruises:

Viking is renowned for its river cruises, including those along the Rhine. They offer guided tours and shore excursions that focus on cultural exploration, history, and local experiences. The company is known for its comfortable ships and knowledgeable guides.

AmaWaterways:

AmaWaterways is another highly regarded river cruise company that operates along the Rhine. They provide guided tours with a focus on personalized experiences, offering diverse excursions that cater to various interests, including culinary, active pursuits, and cultural immersion.

Tauck:

Tauck is known for its all-inclusive river cruises, including those along the Rhine. Their guided tours and shore excursions often emphasize cultural enrichment, with expert guides providing in-depth insights into the destinations visited. Tauck is recognized for its attention to detail and luxury experiences.

Scenic Cruises:

Scenic Cruises offers river cruises along the Rhine, featuring guided tours and excursions that cover a range of interests. The company is known for its innovative itineraries, including exclusive experiences and scenic activities.

Uniworld Boutique River Cruise Collection:

Uniworld offers boutique river cruises with a focus on luxury and personalized service. Their guided tours and shore excursions along the Rhine cater to cultural exploration, and passengers can expect high-quality experiences with attention to detail.

Crystal River Cruises:

Crystal River Cruises provides upscale river cruises along the Rhine, offering guided tours and shore excursions that combine cultural enrichment with luxury experiences.

Their expertly curated excursions often include exclusive access to attractions and personalized activities.

Avalon Waterways:

Avalon Waterways is known for its innovative "Suite Ships" and offers guided tours and shore excursions along the Rhine. They provide a variety of excursions, allowing passengers to customize their experience based on personal interests.

When choosing a guided tour and shore excursion company, it's advisable to read reviews, consider the type of experiences they offer, and ensure they align with your preferences. Additionally, check if the company provides options for various interests, whether it's cultural exploration, culinary experiences, or active pursuits along the Rhine River.

OUTDOOR ADVENTURES ALONG THE RHINE

Embarking on a Rhine River cruise unveils not only a journey through cultural and historical riches but also an array of outdoor adventures that allow travelers to connect with the stunning landscapes and picturesque settings along this iconic waterway.

From invigorating hikes through vineyard-covered hills to serene bicycle rides along riverbanks, the Rhine offers a diverse range of outdoor activities that cater to both the nature enthusiast and the adventure seeker.

Vineyard Hiking Trails:

Immerse yourself in the breathtaking scenery of the Rhine's vineyard-covered hills by exploring the network of hiking trails that wind through these lush landscapes.

The Rheingau region, known for its renowned Riesling wines, offers trails that lead through terraced vineyards, providing panoramic views of the river below.

Hike to vantage points where you can admire the symmetry of the grapevines and the meandering Rhine, creating a perfect fusion of outdoor adventure and natural beauty.

Rhine Gorge Cycling Paths:

Cycling enthusiasts can revel in the joy of pedaling along dedicated cycling paths that run parallel to the Rhine. The Rhine Gorge, a UNESCO World Heritage site, provides a captivating backdrop as you ride through charming villages and vineyard-clad hills.

The level terrain of these paths makes cycling accessible to all skill levels, offering a leisurely way to explore the region's diverse landscapes.

Castle-to-Castle Hikes:

For those seeking a mix of history and adventure, embark on castle-to-castle hikes that take you to the medieval fortresses perched along the Rhine's banks.

Trails such as the Rheinsteig Path offer opportunities to explore iconic castles like Marksburg and Rheinfels while traversing scenic landscapes. The combination of historical exploration and outdoor activity creates a dynamic and immersive experience.

Kayaking and Canoeing Adventures:

Feel the exhilaration of navigating the Rhine's waters by engaging in kayaking or canoeing excursions. Several sections of the river, including the Middle Rhine, provide opportunities for waterborne adventures.

Paddle past charming villages, verdant vineyards, and riverside castles, all while enjoying a unique perspective of the Rhine's beauty.

Riverside Yoga and Wellness Retreats:

Indulge in wellness-focused outdoor activities with riverside yoga sessions and wellness retreats. Some cruise lines offer activities that allow passengers to connect with the serene ambiance of the Rhine's banks through yoga or meditation sessions.

Enjoy stretching and relaxation amid the scenic surroundings, creating a holistic and rejuvenating experience.

Guided Nature Walks:

Embark on guided nature walks that lead you through the Rhine's diverse landscapes, from riverside promenades to forested trails.

Knowledgeable guides provide insights into the local flora and fauna, as well as the cultural and historical significance of the region.These walks offer a harmonious blend of exploration and education amid the natural splendor of the Rhine.

Hot Air Balloon Adventures:

Elevate your outdoor adventure with a hot air balloon ride that provides a bird's-eye view of the Rhine's picturesque landscapes.

Drift above vineyards, castles, and charming towns, taking in the scenic panorama from the sky. This unique perspective offers a sense of tranquility and awe-inspiring beauty.

Lakeside Retreats and Picnics:

Discover serene lakeside retreats along the Rhine, where you can unwind and enjoy picnics amid nature.

Some cruise itineraries include stops at lakeside locations, providing passengers with opportunities to relax by the water, indulge in a picnic, or simply soak in the peaceful ambiance of the surrounding landscapes.

RELAXATION AND WELLNESS OPTIONS

From onboard spa experiences to riverside yoga sessions, the Rhine offers a variety of options for those seeking rejuvenation and tranquility.

Spa and Wellness Facilities Onboard:

Many cruise ships sailing the Rhine River are equipped with onboard spa and wellness facilities. Pamper yourself with massages, facials, and soothing treatments designed to relax both the body and mind.

Unwind in saunas, steam rooms, or enjoy a dip in the onboard pool, all while sailing along the serene Rhine.

Riverside Yoga and Meditation:

Participate in rejuvenating yoga and meditation sessions held on the ship's deck or along the riverside. Imagine the soothing sound of the flowing Rhine as you engage in mindfulness practices, allowing the tranquil surroundings to enhance your wellness journey.

Scenic Sun Deck Lounging:

Take advantage of the scenic sun decks on the cruise ship to bask in the sun, read a book, or simply enjoy the breathtaking views. Lounge chairs and cozy corners provide the perfect setting for relaxation, allowing you to soak up the serene ambiance of the Rhine's landscapes.

Spa Town Visits:

Explore spa towns along the Rhine, such as Baden-Baden, where thermal baths and wellness centers abound. Treat yourself to a day of relaxation in the healing waters of natural springs or indulge in spa treatments that draw on centuries-old traditions. These towns offer a serene escape for those seeking therapeutic wellness experiences.

Serene Shore Excursions:

Customize your shore excursions to include serene and nature-focused activities. Opt for guided walks through botanical gardens, visit peaceful parks, or explore tranquil lakeside retreats. These excursions provide opportunities to connect with nature and unwind in picturesque settings along the Rhine.

Mindful River Cruising:

Choose cruise lines that offer mindful river cruising experiences. Some companies provide wellness-focused itineraries that include yoga classes, healthy dining options, and expert-led sessions on mindfulness. Delight in the slow pace of the river journey, allowing you to fully immerse yourself in the tranquility of the Rhine.

Onboard Fitness Classes:

Engage in onboard fitness classes to maintain your well-being while cruising. Many ships offer fitness programs, including group classes and personal training sessions.

Whether it's a morning stretch or a high-energy workout, these options cater to those who prioritize health and wellness during their Rhine River adventure.

Quiet Reading Nooks:

Discover quiet reading nooks on the ship where you can unwind with a good book. The gentle motion of the ship and the scenic views provide a serene backdrop for relaxation.

Whether indoors or on a secluded deck, these nooks offer a peaceful escape for those seeking quiet moments along the Rhine.

Holistic Wellness Lectures:

Enjoy holistic wellness lectures onboard that cover topics such as nutrition, stress management, and overall well-being.

Expert speakers may provide insights and tips to enhance your physical and mental health, contributing to a holistic wellness experience during your Rhine River cruise.

Customized Spa Packages:

Check if cruise lines offer customizable spa packages that cater to individual preferences. Whether you prefer massages, facial treatments, or other wellness services, inquire about options to tailor your spa experience and make it uniquely suited to your relaxation needs.

Chapter Nine
ONBOARD EXPERIENCE
TYPES OF RHINE RIVER CRUISE SHIPS

Longships: A Blend of Innovation and Tradition

Embarking on a Rhine River cruise aboard a Viking Longship is an extraordinary journey that seamlessly blends innovation with tradition, offering passengers a distinctive and immersive experience along the iconic waterway.

The Viking Longships represent a modern marvel in river cruising, combining cutting-edge design, comfort, and a nod to the rich maritime history that has shaped the culture along the Rhine.

Innovative Design:

Viking Longships are renowned for their innovative design, featuring a sleek and streamlined exterior that effortlessly navigates the Rhine's waters.

The ships' long, narrow shape allows for easy maneuvering through locks and under bridges, ensuring a smooth and uninterrupted journey along the river. This design innovation maximizes both efficiency and passenger comfort.

Panoramic Views and Sun Decks:

One of the hallmarks of Viking Longships is their focus on providing passengers with breathtaking panoramic views of the scenic landscapes along the Rhine.

Expansive windows adorn the ship's common areas and staterooms, allowing guests to enjoy the ever-changing scenery from the comfort of their surroundings. The spacious sun decks further enhance this experience, providing open-air spaces for relaxation and sightseeing.

Aquavit Terrace:

An iconic feature of Viking Longships is the innovative Aquavit Terrace, a unique indoor-outdoor lounge located at the ship's bow. This multi-functional space seamlessly connects with the surrounding environment, offering an ideal spot for al fresco dining, socializing, or simply enjoying the fresh Rhine air.

The Aquavit Terrace embodies the ship's commitment to providing passengers with an immersive and engaging onboard experience.

Scandinavian Elegance:

Step onboard a Viking Longship, and you'll be enveloped in the understated elegance of Scandinavian design. Clean lines, neutral tones, and thoughtful touches create an atmosphere of modern sophistication.

The interiors are tastefully adorned with contemporary artworks and Viking-inspired decor, paying homage to the maritime heritage that inspired the creation of these ships.

Stateroom Comfort and Efficiency:

Viking Longships prioritize passenger comfort with thoughtfully designed staterooms that balance efficiency and luxury. Ingenious storage solutions and efficient layouts ensure that every inch of space is utilized effectively.

Guests can unwind in well-appointed cabins that feature modern amenities, including comfortable beds, spacious bathrooms, and interactive entertainment systems.

Culinary Excellence:

Onboard dining is an integral part of the Viking Longship experience, emphasizing culinary excellence with a focus on regional flavors. The main dining room provides a refined atmosphere for gourmet meals, while the Aquavit Terrace offers a more casual dining setting with panoramic views.

The onboard chefs often incorporate local ingredients, allowing passengers to savor the culinary delights of the Rhine region.

Educational Enrichment:

Viking Longships go beyond providing a scenic journey; they offer educational enrichment opportunities that enhance the overall experience.

Onboard lectures, presentations, and cultural performances provide insights into the history, art, and traditions of the regions along the Rhine. Passengers have the opportunity to deepen their understanding of the destinations they explore.

Sustainable Practices:

Reflecting a commitment to environmental responsibility, Viking Longships incorporate sustainable practices into their operation.

From energy-efficient engines to eco-friendly amenities, these ships strive to minimize their impact on the environment.

Passengers can cruise the Rhine with the assurance that their journey aligns with sustainable principles.

Technological Advancements:

Viking Longships seamlessly integrate technological advancements to enhance the onboard experience. From interactive maps that provide real-time information about the journey to onboard Wi-Fi for staying connected, these ships balance tradition with modern conveniences, ensuring that passengers enjoy a seamless and technologically savvy cruise.

Immersive Excursions:

Viking Longships offer a range of immersive shore excursions that allow passengers to explore the cultural gems along the Rhine.

Guided tours, culinary experiences, and hands-on activities provide a deeper understanding of the destinations visited. The ship's innovative design facilitates easy embarkation and disembarkation, ensuring that passengers can make the most of their time ashore.

Riverboats: Navigating Elegance

Embarking on a Rhine River cruise aboard a riverboat is an enchanting experience that navigates the waters with a graceful blend of elegance and intimacy. These vessels, often characterized by their smaller size and charming design, offer passengers a more personalized and immersive journey along the iconic waterway.

From the gentle lapping of the river against the hull to the panoramic views of vineyard-covered hills, riverboats create an atmosphere that resonates with both elegance and a sense of timeless exploration.

Intimate Atmosphere:

Riverboats, in contrast to larger cruise ships, evoke an intimate and cozy atmosphere. With a limited number of cabins and communal spaces, passengers enjoy a more personalized experience, fostering a sense of camaraderie and connection.

The smaller size allows riverboats to navigate narrower sections of the Rhine, reaching charming ports and hidden gems that may be inaccessible to larger vessels.

Scenic Panoramas:

Designed to maximize the enjoyment of the breathtaking Rhine landscapes, riverboats feature large windows and open-air decks that provide panoramic views of the riverbanks.

Passengers can relax in the comfort of their cabins or on the sun deck, immersing themselves in the ever-changing scenery of vineyards, castles, and picturesque towns along the river.

Authentic Design:

Riverboats often embrace an authentic design that reflects the elegance of classic river cruising. With graceful lines, wooden accents, and a charming exterior, these vessels pay homage to the rich maritime heritage of European rivers.

The design creates an ambiance of timeless elegance, allowing passengers to feel a connection to the storied past of river travel.

Culinary Delights:

The dining experience on riverboats is a culinary journey that celebrates the flavors of the Rhine region. Aboard these vessels, passengers can savor gourmet meals crafted with locally sourced ingredients.

The intimate dining spaces provide a relaxed and sophisticated setting, enhancing the overall culinary experience as passengers indulge in the regional delights of the Rhine.

Shore Excursions and Accessibility:

Riverboats excel in providing access to smaller ports and harbors along the Rhine, allowing for a more immersive exploration of the region.

Passengers can easily disembark for shore excursions that delve into the cultural and historical treasures of each destination. This accessibility enhances the overall experience, offering a closer connection to the communities along the riverbanks.

Cozy Cabins and Suites:

Accommodations on riverboats are designed for comfort and intimacy. Cabins and suites are thoughtfully appointed, providing cozy retreats with modern amenities. The smaller number of cabins contributes to a more exclusive and tranquil onboard environment, ensuring that passengers feel at home as they navigate the Rhine's waters.

Relaxing Common Spaces:

Riverboats feature inviting common spaces where passengers can unwind, socialize, and enjoy the leisurely pace of river cruising.

Lounges with panoramic views, libraries, and open-air decks create a relaxed environment for passengers to appreciate the serenity of the Rhine. These common spaces become hubs of relaxation and connection.

Onboard Enrichment Programs:

To enhance the cultural experience, riverboats often offer onboard enrichment programs. Expert lectures, wine tastings, and performances bring the history and traditions of the Rhine to life.

Passengers have the opportunity to engage with knowledgeable guides and local experts, deepening their understanding of the destinations visited.

Personalized Service:

With a smaller guest capacity, riverboats provide a higher level of personalized service. Crew members often get to know passengers by name, creating a warm and welcoming atmosphere. The attentive service contributes to a sense of luxury and ensures that passengers' needs are met with care and consideration.

Evening Entertainment and Stargazing:

Evenings aboard riverboats are enchanting affairs, with opportunities for intimate entertainment and stargazing. From onboard performances to relaxing under the night sky on the open decks, passengers can embrace the tranquility and romance of the Rhine after sunset.

Boutique Cruises: Personalized Intimacy

Embarking on a Rhine River cruise aboard a boutique cruise vessel promises a voyage characterized by personalized intimacy, curated experiences, and a distinct sense of charm.

Boutique cruises redefine the traditional river cruising experience, offering a more exclusive and tailored journey for those seeking a refined exploration of the Rhine.

From luxurious accommodations to unique itineraries, these vessels prioritize individualized attention, creating an atmosphere where passengers can immerse themselves in the romance and cultural richness of the iconic waterway.

Exclusivity in Design:

Boutique cruise vessels along the Rhine are distinguished by their exclusive and thoughtfully designed interiors. The emphasis is on creating an ambiance of sophistication and comfort, with carefully selected furnishings, stylish décor, and an overall aesthetic that reflects a commitment to providing a refined experience for every passenger.

Limited Passenger Capacity:

What sets boutique cruises apart is their intentionally limited passenger capacity. With fewer guests onboard, passengers can enjoy a more spacious and tranquil environment.

This exclusivity allows for a higher level of personalized service, ensuring that each traveler's needs and preferences are attentively catered to throughout the journey.

Gourmet Dining Experiences:

Culinary excellence is a hallmark of boutique cruises on the Rhine. These vessels often boast gourmet dining experiences, featuring carefully crafted menus that showcase regional flavors and highlight the culinary richness of the Rhine.

Intimate dining spaces and attentive service contribute to an indulgent journey for food enthusiasts.

Unique Itineraries and Hidden Gems:

Boutique cruises are known for offering unique itineraries that go beyond the usual tourist paths. Passengers have the opportunity to explore hidden gems along the Rhine, discovering charming villages, lesser-known landmarks, and cultural treasures that may be overlooked by larger vessels. This focus on authenticity adds a layer of discovery to the cruise experience.

Personalized Shore Excursions:

Shore excursions are curated to provide a more personalized and immersive exploration of the destinations visited. Boutique cruise lines often offer small-group tours led by knowledgeable guides, allowing passengers to engage more intimately with the local culture, history, and traditions of the Rhine region.

Luxurious Accommodations:

Boutique cruise vessels prioritize luxurious accommodations that redefine onboard comfort. Spacious suites, premium amenities, and elegant design elements create an environment of opulence.

The emphasis on quality extends to every detail, ensuring that passengers experience the epitome of luxury during their Rhine River cruise.

Spa and Wellness Retreats:

Many boutique cruises feature spa and wellness retreats, providing passengers with opportunities for relaxation and rejuvenation while cruising the Rhine.

From onboard spa facilities to wellness-focused activities, these vessels cater to those seeking a holistic and indulgent experience amid the scenic beauty of the river.

Personalized Service:

The hallmark of boutique cruises is the unparalleled level of personalized service. The onboard staff is dedicated to creating a warm and welcoming atmosphere, with attention to individual preferences.

From remembering guests' names to anticipating their needs, the crew ensures that each passenger feels truly valued and cared for throughout the journey.

Intimate Common Spaces:

Boutique cruise vessels feature intimate common spaces where passengers can gather, relax, and socialize. Stylish lounges, cozy libraries, and panoramic decks contribute to a sense of community among travelers.

These spaces become hubs of connection, where passengers can share their experiences and create lasting memories.

Romantic Evenings and Entertainment:

Evenings aboard boutique cruises are characterized by a romantic ambiance and curated entertainment. From live music performances to themed events, passengers can indulge in the enchanting atmosphere of the Rhine under the starlit sky. The focus on creating memorable evenings adds a touch of magic to the overall cruise experience.

Luxury Cruises: Opulence on the Water

Embarking on a luxury Rhine River cruise is an opulent sojourn that epitomizes sophistication, impeccable service, and a heightened level of comfort.

These cruises redefine the concept of indulgence, creating an environment where every detail is meticulously curated to exceed the expectations of discerning travelers.

From lavish accommodations to gourmet dining experiences, luxury cruises along the Rhine offer a sublime fusion of sumptuousness and cultural exploration.

Lavish Accommodations:

Luxury Rhine River cruises boast opulent accommodations, often featuring spacious suites with panoramic views of the river.

Lavish furnishings, premium linens, and elegant design elements create an atmosphere of refined comfort.

Guests are enveloped in a world of luxury as they retreat to their private havens after a day of exploration.

Gourmet Dining Experiences:

Culinary excellence is at the heart of luxury river cruising. Passengers indulge in gourmet dining experiences that showcase the finest regional and international cuisines.

Expert chefs craft meticulously curated menus, complemented by an extensive selection of wines. Whether dining in elegant onboard restaurants or al fresco settings, each meal becomes a gastronomic journey along the Rhine.

Personalized Service:

Luxury cruises prioritize personalized service to an unparalleled degree. A dedicated and attentive staff ensures that every need is met with grace and efficiency. From the moment guests step aboard, they are treated to a level of service that anticipates their desires, creating an atmosphere of seamless luxury throughout the cruise.

Exclusive Shore Excursions:

Shore excursions on luxury cruises are curated for an exclusive and immersive experience. Small-group tours led by expert guides delve into the cultural, historical, and artistic treasures along the Rhine.

Private visits to landmarks, VIP access to attractions, and tailor-made experiences ensure that passengers enjoy a truly privileged exploration of each destination.

Panoramic Lounges and Observation Decks:

Luxury vessels feature panoramic lounges and observation decks that offer unrivaled views of the Rhine's scenic landscapes.

Passengers can unwind in stylish surroundings, enjoying the ever-changing panorama as the ship gracefully navigates the river. These elevated spaces become sanctuaries of tranquility and beauty.

Onboard Enrichment Programs:

To enhance the cultural experience, luxury cruises often feature onboard enrichment programs. Renowned guest speakers, expert lecturers, and performances by local artists provide passengers with insights into the history, art, and traditions of the Rhine region. These programs add an intellectual and artistic dimension to the journey.

Spa and Wellness Retreats:

Indulgence extends to spa and wellness retreats onboard luxury Rhine River cruises. State-of-the-art spa facilities offer a haven of relaxation, with treatments inspired by both traditional and modern wellness practices. Passengers can rejuvenate body and mind amid the serene beauty of the river.

Exclusive Events and Entertainment:

Luxury cruises often host exclusive events and entertainment tailored to the tastes of discerning travelers. From private concerts to themed soirées, passengers are treated to intimate and sophisticated gatherings that complement the overall ambiance of opulence on the water.

Artfully Designed Interiors:

The interiors of luxury river cruise ships are artfully designed, combining classic elegance with modern sophistication.

Stylish lounges, upscale restaurants, and chic staterooms create an ambiance of refined indulgence. Each space is thoughtfully curated to provide an environment that resonates with luxury and taste.

Customizable Itineraries:

Luxury cruises offer a level of flexibility and customization in itineraries. Passengers can tailor their journeys to include private tours, exclusive experiences, and personalized activities.

This customization ensures that each traveler's preferences and interests are seamlessly integrated into their Rhine River cruise.

CABIN SELECTION AND AMENITIES

Choosing the right cabin on your Rhine River cruise is a crucial aspect of ensuring a comfortable and enjoyable experience.

Different cabin categories and amenities can significantly impact your journey. Here's a guide to help you make informed decisions when selecting your cabin and exploring onboard amenities:

Cabin Categories:

Interior Cabins:

Ideal for those on a budget, interior cabins provide a cozy retreat without windows. Perfect for passengers who prioritize spending more time exploring onshore.

Oceanview Cabins:

These cabins offer windows or portholes, providing natural light and limited views. They are a mid-range option for those seeking a balance between budget and views.

Balcony Cabins:

Balcony cabins provide a private outdoor space, allowing you to enjoy the scenic beauty of the Rhine from the comfort of your cabin. Perfect for those who value panoramic views and fresh air.

Suite Accommodations:

Suites offer more space, enhanced amenities, and often additional perks. They are suitable for travelers seeking a more luxurious and spacious onboard experience.

Location Matters:

  - Consider the location of your cabin within the ship. Cabins toward the center and lower decks may experience less movement, suitable for passengers prone to seasickness.

- Cabins on higher decks often offer better views, but they may be more susceptible to movement. Choose based on your preferences and tolerance for motion.

Amenities and Inclusions:

- Private Bathrooms: Ensure your chosen cabin category includes a private bathroom with essential amenities. Some suites may offer upgraded bathroom facilities.

- Storage Space: Evaluate the storage space available in the cabin. Efficient storage is essential for staying organized during the cruise.

- Entertainment Systems: Check for in-cabin entertainment systems, including TV, movies, and music options. These can enhance your relaxation during downtime.

- Climate Control: Ensure cabins have climate control options to maintain a comfortable environment, especially during different seasons along the Rhine.

- Wi-Fi Access: Confirm the availability of onboard Wi-Fi if staying connected is important to you. Some cruise lines offer complimentary or paid internet access.

Special Cabin Features:

- Connecting Cabins: Ideal for families or groups traveling together, connecting cabins provide shared access between two adjacent cabins.

- Accessible Cabins: If you have mobility concerns, inquire about accessible cabins that are designed to accommodate passengers with disabilities.

Onboard Amenities:

- Dining Options: Explore the onboard dining options, including formal dining rooms, casual eateries, and specialty restaurants. Consider any dietary preferences or restrictions.

- Lounges and Bars: Check for lounges and bars onboard where you can relax, socialize, and enjoy beverages with fellow passengers.

- Wellness Facilities: Some cruise lines offer wellness amenities such as fitness centers, spas, and wellness programs. Consider these options for relaxation and self-care.

- Entertainment Venues: Look into the onboard entertainment options, which may include theaters, live performances, and enrichment programs.

Balcony Considerations:

- If you choose a balcony cabin, consider the size and layout of the balcony. Some balconies may be more spacious, allowing for comfortable outdoor seating.

- Verify if your chosen itinerary and season make a balcony worthwhile. Weather conditions may impact the utility of the balcony during certain times.

Cruise Line Reputation:

- Research the reputation of the cruise line regarding cabin comfort, service quality, and overall guest satisfaction. Reviews from previous passengers can provide valuable insights.

Ultimately, your cabin choice depends on your preferences, budget, and the type of experience you seek. Consider what amenities and features are most important to you, and ensure that your cabin selection aligns with your expectations for a delightful Rhine River cruise.

DINING AND ENTERTAINMENT

Dining and entertainment are integral aspects of the Rhine River cruise experience, enhancing your journey with culinary delights and engaging activities.

Dining

Main Dining Room:

- Most Rhine River cruises feature a main dining room where passengers can enjoy daily meals. This is typically included in the cruise fare.

- Expect a variety of dishes, often inspired by regional flavors along the Rhine. Menus may include both international and local cuisine.

Specialty Restaurants:

- Some cruise lines offer specialty restaurants that provide a more intimate dining experience. These may focus on gourmet cuisine, themed dinners, or specific culinary styles.

- Specialty restaurants often require reservations and may have an additional fee.

Al Fresco Dining:

- Take advantage of al fresco dining options, especially if your ship has outdoor spaces. Enjoy meals with scenic views as you cruise along the Rhine.

Local Cuisine:

- Explore the flavors of the region with meals that highlight local ingredients and specialties. Rhine River cruises often incorporate regional cuisine into their menus.

Flexible Dining Times:

- Check if your cruise offers flexible dining times, allowing you to choose when to dine. This flexibility can be convenient for passengers with varied schedules.

Culinary Events:

- Some cruises host special culinary events such as wine tastings, chef's dinners, and local food-themed nights. Participate in these events to enhance your gastronomic experience.

Entertainment

Live Performances:

- Enjoy live performances onboard, which may include musical acts, dance performances, and themed shows. Check the entertainment schedule for nightly offerings.

Cultural Enrichment Programs:

- Many Rhine River cruises incorporate cultural enrichment programs. These may feature lectures, talks, and demonstrations by experts, providing insights into the history and culture of the regions you visit.

Themed Nights:

- Experience themed nights that celebrate the destinations along the Rhine. From costume parties to regional music events, these themed nights add a fun and festive element to the cruise.

Onboard Bars and Lounges:

- Relax in onboard bars and lounges, which often host social events and offer a variety of beverages. Enjoy the camaraderie of fellow passengers while taking in scenic views.

Movie Nights:

- Some cruises organize movie nights, allowing passengers to enjoy films under the stars or in designated onboard theaters. Check the schedule for cinematic offerings.

Interactive Activities:

- Participate in interactive activities such as trivia nights, cooking classes, or wine tastings. These activities foster a sense of community and engagement.

Observation Decks:

- Spend time on the ship's observation decks, especially during scenic cruising along the Rhine. Take in the landscapes and capture memorable moments.

Wellness Programs:

- Explore wellness programs that may include fitness classes, yoga sessions, and spa services. Relax and rejuvenate while cruising along the river.

Nightly Entertainment Shows:

- Experience nightly entertainment shows that showcase the talents of onboard performers. These may include musicals, variety shows, and themed performances.

Social Spaces:

- Take advantage of social spaces onboard, such as lounges and gathering areas. These spaces provide opportunities to connect with fellow passengers and share experiences.

Chapter Ten

PRACTICAL TIPS FOR RHINE RIVER TRAVEL

TRANSPORTATION TO AND FROM PORTS

Air Travel Considerations

Choosing Arrival and Departure Airports

Proximity to Port: Select airports that are conveniently located in proximity to your embarkation and disembarkation ports. This minimizes travel time and stress, allowing you to start and end your cruise with ease.

Major Hubs: Consider using major international hubs that offer a variety of flight options. Popular airports near the Rhine include Amsterdam Schiphol, Frankfurt Airport, and Zurich Airport.

Timing and Arrival Day

Arrival Timing: Plan your arrival for the day before your cruise departure. This provides a buffer in case of flight delays or unforeseen circumstances, reducing the risk of missing the cruise.

Overnight Stay: Consider booking a hotel for the night before embarkation. This allows you to rest, adjust to any time zone differences, and explore the departure city.

Ground Transportation

Transfer Options: Research transportation options from the airport to the cruise port. Some cruise lines offer transfer services, or you may choose taxis, shuttles, or public transportation based on your preferences and budget.

Pre-book Transfers: If available, consider pre-booking transfers with the cruise line or a reputable transportation service to ensure a smooth transition from the airport to the port.

Departure Day Logistics

Disembarkation Timing: For departure, aim for flights in the afternoon or evening to allow ample time to disembark, clear customs (if applicable), and travel to the airport without rushing.

Post-Cruise Exploration: If time permits, plan a post-cruise exploration of the disembarkation city before your flight. This adds an extra layer of enjoyment to your travel experience.

Flight Flexibility

Flexible Tickets: consider purchasing flexible or refundable airfare, especially if there's uncertainty in your travel plans. This provides flexibility in case of unexpected changes or delays.

Travel Insurance: Explore travel insurance options that cover trip cancellations, interruptions, or delays. Having insurance can offer peace of mind and financial protection.

Security and Customs

Airport Security: Be mindful of security procedures and arrive at the airport with ample time for check-in and security checks. Ensure compliance with current travel regulations.

Customs and Immigration: Understand the customs and immigration procedures at both your departure and arrival airports. Some flights may involve connecting in different countries, each with its own entry requirements.

Packing Strategically

Carry-On Essentials: Pack essential items, including travel documents, medications, a change of clothes, and important valuables, in your carry-on bag. This ensures you have immediate access to crucial items even if checked luggage is delayed.

Time Zone Adjustments

Jet Lag Considerations: If your Rhine River cruise involves multiple time zones, consider adjusting your sleep schedule before departure to minimize the impact of jet lag. Stay hydrated and expose yourself to natural light upon arrival.

Airport Lounge Access:

Lounge Memberships: If you have a long layover or arrive early at the airport, consider purchasing access to airport lounges. Lounges provide a comfortable and quiet space to relax, enjoy refreshments, and access amenities.

Communication and Documentation:

Emergency Contacts: Share your travel itinerary and emergency contacts with someone you trust. Having a point of contact aware of your plans can be helpful in case of unforeseen events.

Digital Copies: Carry digital copies of essential documents such as your passport, cruise confirmation, and flight details. Store these in secure cloud storage for easy access in case of loss or theft.

Pre-Cruise Transportation Planning

Pre-cruise transportation planning is a crucial step in ensuring a smooth and enjoyable journey to your Rhine River cruise. From choosing the right mode of transportation to considering logistics, here's a comprehensive guide to help you navigate the pre-cruise phase:

Selecting the Arrival City

Proximity to Cruise Port: Choose an arrival city that is in close proximity to the cruise port. This minimizes travel time on the day of embarkation, allowing for a more relaxed start to your cruise.

Air Travel Considerations

Arrival Timing: Plan your arrival for at least a day before your cruise departure. This provides a buffer in case of flight delays or unexpected disruptions, reducing the risk of missing the cruise.

Airport Selection: Opt for airports with good transportation links to the cruise port. Major international hubs near the Rhine include Amsterdam Schiphol, Frankfurt Airport, and Zurich Airport.

Ground Transportation

Transfer Options: Research transportation options from the airport to the cruise port. Some cruise lines offer transfer services, or you may choose taxis, shuttles, or public transportation based on your preferences and budget.

Pre-book Transfers: If available, consider pre-booking transfers with the cruise line or a reputable transportation service to ensure a seamless transition from the airport to the port.

Train or Bus Travel

European Rail Network: If you are in Europe or arriving from nearby cities, consider using the extensive European rail network. Trains often provide a convenient and scenic mode of transportation.

Coach Services: Long-distance bus services, such as FlixBus or Eurolines, may be cost-effective options for reaching cities along the Rhine.

Private Car Services

Car Rentals: If you prefer flexibility, renting a car allows you to explore the region at your own pace. Ensure that your chosen rental company has convenient drop-off locations near the cruise port.

Private Car Services: Consider hiring a private car service for a comfortable and stress-free journey. This option is particularly convenient if traveling with luggage or a group.

Hotel Stay Considerations:

Pre-Cruise Hotel: Book a hotel for the night before embarkation. This not only provides a restful stay but also allows you to explore the departure city, adding an extra dimension to your travel experience.

Hotel Transportation: Inquire if the hotel offers transportation services to the cruise port. Some hotels have partnerships with cruise lines and provide dedicated shuttles.

Local Transportation Apps:

Ride-Sharing Services: Utilize ride-sharing services like Uber or local alternatives for convenient transportation within the city or between the hotel and cruise port.

Public Transportation Apps: Familiarize yourself with public transportation options using apps that provide real-time schedules and route information.

Cruise Line Transfers

Cruise Line Services: Check if your cruise line offers transfer services from designated pick-up points, such as airports or hotels. These services are often coordinated to align with embarkation times.

Navigation Apps and Maps

Navigation Apps: Download navigation apps that can guide you from your arrival point to the cruise port. These apps can provide real-time directions and help you navigate efficiently.

Stay Informed About Local Events

Local Events: Check for any local events or road closures that may impact transportation on your travel dates. Staying informed about potential disruptions ensures that you can plan alternative routes if needed.

Ground Transportation Options

Navigating ground transportation is a key component of planning your Rhine River cruise, ensuring a smooth journey from your arrival point to the cruise port.

Here's a guide to various ground transportation options, allowing you to choose the mode that best suits your preferences and travel needs:

Cruise Line Transfers

Many cruise lines offer transfer services from major airports or designated pick-up points to the cruise port. These services are often convenient, providing a hassle-free transition to the embarkation point.

Advantages:

Coordination with cruise line schedules, assistance with luggage, and a streamlined process from arrival to the cruise terminal.

Considerations:

Check availability, schedule, and pricing for cruise line transfer services. It's advisable to pre-book these services to secure your spot.

Taxis:

Taxis are readily available at airports and in city centers. They provide a direct and private mode of transportation to the cruise port.

Advantages:

Convenience, door-to-door service, and flexibility in departure times.

Considerations:

Confirm taxi availability and rates at your arrival point. Be aware of potential surcharges during peak hours.

Private Car Services

Private car services, including car rentals with chauffeurs, offer a personalized and comfortable travel experience.

Advantages:

Privacy, comfort, and flexibility. Chauffeurs can assist with luggage and provide a tailored journey.

Considerations:

Pre-book services with reputable companies. Clarify rates, inclusions, and any additional charges in advance.

Ride-Sharing Services

Ride-sharing services like Uber or local alternatives operate in many cities, providing convenient transportation at the tap of a smartphone.

Advantages:

Cost-effective, easily accessible, and real-time tracking of your ride. Payment is typically handled electronically.

Considerations:

Check the availability and regulations of ride-sharing services in the city or country you are visiting.

Public Transportation:

Public transportation, including buses, trams, and trains, can be an affordable and efficient way to reach the cruise port.

Advantages:

Cost-effective, often well-connected, and an opportunity to experience local commuting.

Considerations:

Familiarize yourself with the public transportation system in advance. Verify schedules and routes to ensure compatibility with your cruise schedule.

Hotel Shuttles:

Some hotels near cruise ports offer shuttle services for guests. These shuttles may provide transportation directly to the cruise terminal.

Advantages:

Convenience for guests staying at partner hotels, potentially reducing the need for additional ground transportation.

Considerations:

Inquire about the availability, schedule, and any associated fees for hotel shuttle services.

Rental Cars:

Renting a car provides flexibility in exploring the region before or after your cruise. Car rental agencies are typically available at airports.

Advantages:

Independence, the ability to explore at your own pace, and convenience for travelers with specific itineraries.

Considerations:

Ensure drop-off locations are available near the cruise port. Be aware of parking availability and costs.

Limousine Services:

Limousine services offer a luxurious and comfortable mode of transportation. They often cater to specific travel preferences.

Advantages:

Comfort, personalized service, and a touch of luxury for special occasions.

Considerations:

Pre-book reputable limousine services, verify rates, and communicate any specific requirements.

Walking or Biking

Depending on the proximity of your accommodation to the cruise port, walking or biking might be viable options, especially in city centers.

Advantages:

Environmentally friendly, cost-free, and a chance to enjoy the surroundings on foot or by bicycle.

Considerations:

Assess the distance and local infrastructure. Ensure safe pathways for walking or biking.

Local Tourist Transportation

Description:

Some cities offer tourist transportation options, such as sightseeing buses or boats. These may provide both transportation and an introduction to local attractions.

Advantages:

A combination of transportation and a guided tour experience.

Considerations:

Explore options available at your arrival destination. Check schedules and routes.

Self-Drive and Parking Facilities

Self-driving to the cruise port can be a convenient and flexible option, providing you with control over your schedule and the ability to explore the region at your own pace. Here's a guide to self-drive and parking facilities for your Rhine River cruise:

Renting a Car

Car Rental Agencies: Choose reputable car rental agencies available at your arrival city or airport. Major companies typically operate in well-connected locations.

Booking in Advance: To secure the best rates and ensure availability, consider booking your rental car in advance. Online platforms often offer competitive prices.

Driving to the Cruise Port

Navigation Apps: Use navigation apps to plan your route from your arrival point to the cruise port. Ensure the apps are updated with real-time traffic information.

Local Road Regulations: Familiarize yourself with local road regulations, traffic signs, and parking rules in the region you'll be driving through.

Parking at the Cruise Port

Onsite Cruise Port Parking: Many cruise ports offer onsite parking facilities. Check with your cruise line or the port authority to confirm the availability, pricing, and reservation options.

Offsite Parking Lots: Explore offsite parking lots near the cruise port. Some private parking facilities provide shuttle services to and from the port.

Hotel Parking: If staying at a hotel near the cruise port, inquire about parking options. Some hotels offer secure parking for guests, sometimes at a reduced rate.

Parking Reservations

Pre-Booking: Consider pre-booking your parking space, especially if the cruise port is known for high demand. This ensures availability and sometimes comes with discounted rates.

Online Platforms: Utilize online platforms that specialize in cruise port parking reservations. These platforms often provide information on available lots, pricing, and customer reviews.

Parking Costs:

Daily or Flat Rate: Parking costs can vary, typically charged on a daily or flat rate basis. Some cruise lines may offer packages that include parking with the cruise fare.

Discounts and Promotions: Look for discounts or promotions on parking fees, especially when booking in advance or as part of a cruise package.

Security and Amenities

Security Measures: Choose parking facilities with adequate security measures, such as surveillance cameras or personnel on-site. Ensuring the safety of your vehicle is essential.

Shuttle Services: If parking offsite, inquire about shuttle services to the cruise port. Many parking lots offer convenient transportation options to and from the port.

Drop-Off and Pick-Up Procedures

Smooth Transitions: Plan your drop-off and pick-up procedures in advance. Understand the cruise port's layout and designated areas for vehicular traffic to ensure a smooth transition.

Arrival Day Considerations: On the day of embarkation, consider arriving early to allow time for parking, check-in, and security procedures.

Accessibility and Convenience

Proximity to Cruise Terminal: Choose parking facilities that are conveniently located to the cruise terminal. This minimizes the time and effort required to reach the ship.

Accessibility Features: If you have specific accessibility needs, check if the parking facilities offer designated spaces or services to accommodate your requirements.

Alternative Transportation Options

Return Transportation: Plan how you'll return to the parking facility after disembarking. Shuttles, taxis, or ride-sharing services can be viable options.

Exploration Options: If you plan to explore the port city before or after the cruise, having a rental car allows you to do so at your own pace.

Familiarize Yourself with Cruise Line Policies:

Check with your cruise line for any specific guidelines or recommendations regarding self-drive and parking. Some cruise lines may provide detailed information to assist passengers.

EMERGENCY PROCEDURES

Understanding and being prepared for emergency procedures is essential to ensure your safety and well-being during a Rhine River cruise. Cruise lines prioritize passenger safety, and passengers should familiarize themselves with emergency protocols.

Muster Drill:

Attend the mandatory muster drill conducted at the beginning of your cruise. This safety briefing provides important information on emergency procedures, life jacket usage, and evacuation routes.

Listen and Watch: pay close attention to crew instructions during the muster drill. The information provided is crucial in the unlikely event of an emergency.

Emergency Contact Information:

Familiarize yourself with key emergency contacts, including the ship's emergency number, the location of emergency exits, and the meeting point for your muster station.

Save the ship's emergency number on your phone and carry a physical copy of important contact information.

Life Jackets:

Know the location of life jackets in your cabin and throughout the ship. Life jackets are typically stored in cabins, on deck, or in designated areas.

Understand how to properly wear and fasten your life jacket. Crew members are available to assist if needed.

Emergency Alarms:

Familiarize yourself with the ship's emergency alarm signals. Different signals may indicate a fire, abandon ship, or other emergencies.

In the event of an alarm, react promptly to crew instructions. Follow evacuation routes and assemble at your designated muster station.

Evacuation Procedures:

Be aware of evacuation routes and the location of lifeboats. Evacuation procedures are typically outlined in your cabin, and crew members will guide passengers during emergencies.

If possible, assist fellow passengers, especially those with mobility challenges, in reaching safety during an evacuation.

Emergency Equipment:

Familiarize yourself with the location of emergency equipment, such as fire extinguishers and emergency exits, in key areas of the ship.

Do not attempt to use emergency equipment unless you are trained to do so. Notify crew members of any emergency situations.

Emergency Communication:

Pay attention to announcements made through the ship's public address (PA) system. Important information and instructions will be communicated through this system.

Stay informed about the situation by listening to updates and announcements from the ship's captain and crew.

Emergency Services on Board

Medical Facilities: Familiarize yourself with the ship's medical facilities and services. In case of illness or injury, seek assistance from the onboard medical team.

Emergency Response Team: The ship has an emergency response team trained to handle various situations. Follow their instructions in case of emergencies.

Personal Safety Measures

Cabin Safety: Keep your cabin door closed and locked, especially at night or when you're not present. Follow safety guidelines provided by the cruise line.

Emergency Exit Locations: Identify the location of emergency exits near your cabin and throughout the ship.

Stay Calm and Follow Instructions:

In the event of an emergency, stay calm. Panic can hinder the effectiveness of emergency procedures.

Always follow the instructions of the ship's crew. They are trained to handle emergencies and will guide passengers to safety.

By familiarizing yourself with these emergency procedures, you contribute to a safe and secure environment for yourself and fellow passengers during your Rhine River cruise. While emergencies are rare, being

SAFETY AND HEALTH CONSIDERATIONS

Ensuring safety and prioritizing health considerations are paramount for a positive and worry-free Rhine River cruise experience.

Pre-Cruise Health Preparations

Medical Check-up: Consider scheduling a pre-cruise medical check-up, especially if you have underlying health conditions. Discuss travel plans with your healthcare provider.

Prescriptions: Ensure you have an adequate supply of necessary medications for the duration of your cruise.

Cruise Line Health Guidelines:

Familiarize yourself with the health and safety policies of your chosen cruise line. Cruise lines typically provide guidelines regarding onboard health practices and medical facilities.

Vaccination Requirements:

Check if the cruise line has specific vaccination requirements or recommendations for passengers.

Travel Insurance

Comprehensive Coverage: Purchase travel insurance that includes comprehensive health coverage, trip cancellation, and medical evacuation. Confirm the coverage for unexpected events.

Policy Review: Thoroughly review your travel insurance policy to understand its terms and conditions.

Hand Hygiene

Frequent Handwashing: Practice frequent handwashing with soap and water. Hand sanitizers are often available throughout the ship for additional hygiene.

Avoid Touching Face: Minimize touching your face, especially eyes, nose, and mouth, to reduce the risk of transferring germs.

Onboard Health Facilities

Medical Centers: Identify the location of onboard medical facilities. Cruise ships are equipped with medical centers and qualified medical staff to handle minor health concerns.

Emergency Protocols: Familiarize yourself with emergency medical protocols, including how to contact the ship's medical team in case of illness or injury.

Emergency Evacuation Procedures

Muster Drill Attendance: Attend the mandatory muster drill to understand emergency evacuation procedures and the location of life jackets.

Evacuation Routes: Be aware of evacuation routes, lifeboat locations, and assembly points. Follow crew instructions in the event of an emergency.

Dining and Food Safety

Food Hygiene: Choose dining options that prioritize food safety. Onboard restaurants adhere to rigorous hygiene standards.

Special Dietary Needs: Inform the cruise line of any special dietary requirements or food allergies in advance.

Personal Protective Measures

Mask Usage: Follow any mask usage guidelines provided by the cruise line or in adherence to local health recommendations.

Respect Social Distancing: Respect social distancing measures, if implemented, in public areas and during group activities.

Stay Informed

Daily Updates: Pay attention to daily updates and announcements from the ship's captain and crew. Stay informed about any health-related instructions or changes to the itinerary.

Local Health Guidelines: Be aware of local health guidelines at each port of call and follow recommended practices during shore excursions.

Stay Hydrated and Rested

Hydration: Stay hydrated, especially in warmer climates or during physical activities. Carry a reusable water bottle to ensure access to water throughout the cruise.

Prioritize adequate rest to support your overall well-being during the cruise.

Stay Active

Engage in onboard activities and take advantage of wellness facilities to stay active. Many cruise ships offer fitness centers, yoga classes, and other recreational options.

Respect Quarantine and Isolation Procedures:

In the event of illness, respect quarantine or isolation procedures outlined by the ship's medical team. These measures are in place to protect passengers and crew.

Local Health Protocols:

Follow health protocols and guidelines issued by local authorities at each port of call. Adherence to local regulations contributes to the safety of all passengers.

Emergency Contacts:

Share emergency contact information with a trusted person back home. This includes details of your cruise itinerary and how to reach you in case of urgency.

Traveling with Pre-Existing Conditions:

If you have pre-existing health conditions, notify the cruise line in advance. They may provide additional assistance or accommodations as needed.

By prioritizing safety and health considerations, you contribute to a secure and enjoyable cruise experience along the Rhine River. Following guidelines, staying informed, and practicing good hygiene habits ensure that you can focus on the beauty of your journey while minimizing potential health risks.

INTERACTING WITH LOCALS: LANGUAGE AND ETIQUETTE

Interacting with locals along the Rhine River can be a rewarding experience, offering insights into the rich culture and heritage of the region. Here's a guide to navigating language and etiquette to enhance your interactions with locals:

Learn Basic Local Phrases:

Master basic greetings in the local language, such as "hello," "thank you," and "goodbye." Locals appreciate the effort to communicate in their language.

Common Courtesies: Learn phrases like "please" and "excuse me" to convey politeness and respect.

Use Language Apps:

Translation Apps: Consider using language translation apps to assist with communication. These apps can be valuable tools for understanding and expressing yourself in different languages.

English Proficiency

Assess Language Usage: While English is often widely understood in tourist areas, especially along the Rhine River, be mindful of the language proficiency of locals. In more remote locations, locals might not speak English fluently.

Politeness and Etiquette

Respect Local Customs: Familiarize yourself with local customs and etiquette. For example, in some cultures, it's customary to greet people with a handshake or a specific gesture.

Dress Appropriately: Respect local dress codes, particularly when visiting religious or traditional sites. Dressing modestly is often appreciated.

Be Open and Friendly

Approachable Demeanor: Project an open and friendly demeanor. Smile and be receptive to interactions, as locals may be more inclined to engage with approachable individuals.

Cultural Awareness

Research Local Customs: Prior to your trip, research cultural norms and traditions specific to the regions you'll be visiting. Understanding local customs helps you navigate social interactions with sensitivity.

Non-Verbal Cues: Pay attention to non-verbal cues and body language. This can provide valuable insights into the comfort level of your interactions.

Ask for Permission

Photography Etiquette: When taking photographs, especially of people, ask for permission. Respect individuals' privacy and cultural sensitivities regarding photography.

Support Local Businesses

Local Markets and Shops: Engage with local markets and shops. Purchasing from local businesses not only supports the community but also provides opportunities for authentic interactions with locals.

Participate in Local Activities:

Festivals and Events: If your cruise coincides with local festivals or events, participate and immerse yourself in the celebrations. This offers a chance to interact with locals in a vibrant and festive atmosphere.

Be Patient and Understanding:

Language Barriers: Be patient if there are language barriers. Locals often appreciate the effort, and a positive attitude can bridge communication gaps.

Cultural Differences: Understand that cultural differences may influence communication styles. Be adaptable and open-minded in your interactions.

Respect Personal Space

Cultural Variances: Recognize that personal space preferences may vary across cultures. Be mindful of local norms regarding physical proximity during conversations.

Express Gratitude

Express gratitude to locals who extend hospitality or assistance. A simple "thank you" in the local language can leave a positive impression.

Cultural Sensitivity

Exercise respect when visiting religious sites. Follow guidelines, such as removing your shoes or covering your head, as required by local customs.

Follow Environmental Guidelines

When engaging in outdoor activities, follow environmental guidelines. Show respect for natural landscapes and wildlife.

Cultural Exchange

If the opportunity arises, share aspects of your own culture. This can foster a mutual exchange of experiences and create connections with locals.

SOUVENIRS AND MEMENTOS

Collecting souvenirs and mementos is a delightful way to cherish and remember your Rhine River cruise experience.

Local Artisanal Crafts:

  - **Handcrafted Items:** Seek out locally crafted items that showcase the unique artistry of the region. This could include handmade ceramics, textiles, or wooden crafts.

  - **Artisan Markets:** Explore artisan markets in port cities, where you're likely to find a diverse range of handcrafted souvenirs.

Regional Food and Drinks:

  - **Local Delicacies:** Bring back regional food specialties or beverages as souvenirs. Consider items like local chocolates, wines, or artisanal jams.

  - **Food Markets:** Visit local food markets for a variety of culinary delights that capture the essence of the region.

Traditional Clothing and Accessories:

- **Traditional Attire:** Consider purchasing traditional clothing or accessories representative of the local culture. This could be a piece of traditional clothing, jewelry, or headgear.

  - **Boutiques and Specialty Shops:** Explore local boutiques and specialty shops that focus on traditional or handmade fashion items.

Art and Photography:

  - **Local Artwork:** Invest in local artwork, whether it's paintings, prints, or photography. Local artists often capture the beauty and spirit of the region in their creations.

  - **Art Galleries:** Visit art galleries in port cities to discover unique pieces that resonate with your experience.

Souvenirs Reflecting Local History:

  - **Historical Items:** Look for souvenirs that reflect the history and heritage of the region. This could include replica artifacts, historical maps, or books about local history.

  - **Museums and Historical Sites:** Explore museum gift shops near historical sites for educational and meaningful souvenirs.

Nature-inspired Keepsakes:

  - **Botanical Souvenirs:** Collect nature-inspired items such as pressed flowers, botanical prints, or locally made herbal products.

  - **Visit Gardens:** Explore botanical gardens along the Rhine and consider purchasing items related to the local flora.

Nautical and Maritime Themes:

- **Nautical Souvenirs:** Embrace the maritime theme of your cruise with nautical-inspired souvenirs. This could include ship models, anchor-themed jewelry, or maritime artwork.

- **Portside Shops:** Ports often have shops with a maritime focus, offering a variety of related souvenirs.

Customized Items:

- **Personalized Keepsakes:** Consider getting items customized with your name, the date of your cruise, or the ports you visited. This could include personalized jewelry, engraved items, or custom artwork.

- **Local Artisans:** Connect with local artisans who offer customization services for a truly unique souvenir.

Collector's Items:

- **Limited Editions:** Look for limited edition or collector's items related to your cruise. This could include commemorative plates, coins, or stamps specific to the Rhine River.

- **Cruise Line Merchandise:** Cruise lines often offer exclusive merchandise that can serve as memorable collector's items.

Practical and Everyday Items:

- **Useful Souvenirs:** Choose practical items that you can use in your everyday life, such as a reusable shopping bag, a coffee mug, or a keychain.

- **Quality Over Quantity:** Focus on quality rather than quantity, selecting items that have a genuine connection to your experience.

Local Literature and Music:

- **Books:** Purchase books or literature written by local authors, providing insights into the culture and history of the region.

- **Music CDs:** Explore local music and consider bringing home CDs or digital downloads of regional music styles.

Pottery and Ceramics:

- **Local Pottery:** Discover locally made pottery or ceramics that showcase the artistic traditions of the area.

- **Pottery Studios:** Visit pottery studios or workshops for one-of-a-kind pieces crafted by local artisans.

Memories through Photos:

- **Photo Album or Scrapbook:** Create a photo album or scrapbook to capture memories from your Rhine River cruise. Include pictures, ticket stubs, and small souvenirs for a personalized keepsake.

CONCLUSION

FOND FAREWELL ON YOUR RHINE RIVER ADVENTURE

As your Rhine River adventure draws to a close, it's time to bid a fond farewell to the enchanting landscapes, vibrant cultures, and the memories created along the way. Here are some sentiments to express in your farewell:

Gratitude for the Journey:

  - Express gratitude for the incredible journey along the Rhine River.

  - Acknowledge the experiences, sights, and connections that made the adventure unforgettable.

Appreciation for Fellow Travelers:

  - Thank fellow travelers for sharing this remarkable voyage.

  - Highlight the joy of meeting new friends and the camaraderie that enhanced the experience.

Memorable Moments:

  - Reflect on specific moments that will forever hold a place in your heart.

  - Share anecdotes or highlights that defined the richness of the adventure.

Cultural Enrichment:

- Acknowledge the cultural diversity encountered in each port of call.

- Express how the journey has broadened your understanding and appreciation for different traditions.

Scenic Beauty:

- Bid farewell to the breathtaking landscapes, charming villages, and iconic landmarks.

- Describe the visual splendor that left a lasting impression on your soul.

Cruise Crew Appreciation:

- Extend appreciation to the cruise crew for their dedication and hospitality.

- Thank them for their role in ensuring a smooth and enjoyable journey.

Connection with Nature:

- Acknowledge the beauty of navigating the river and the connection with nature it provided.

- Express gratitude for the serene moments and the tranquility of the waterway.

Culinary Delights:

- Thank the culinary teams for the delectable journey through local flavors.

- Reflect on the culinary experiences that added a savory layer to the overall adventure.

Personal Growth:

- Share how the Rhine River adventure contributed to personal growth and self-discovery.

- Highlight any newfound perspectives or insights gained during the journey.

Farewell to Ports:

- Bid farewell to the ports of call, each with its own charm and character.

- Express hope for future visits and continued exploration.

Promise to Return:

- Leave the door open for future adventures along the Rhine River or other waterways.

- Express the desire to return and explore more of the enchanting destinations.

Wishes for Safe Journeys:

- Extend heartfelt wishes for safe journeys to fellow travelers.

- Express hope that the memories created on the Rhine River will be cherished for a lifetime.

Acknowledgment of Crew's Efforts:

- Acknowledge the hard work and dedication of the cruise crew.

- Thank them for creating a welcoming and memorable environment throughout the journey.

Embracing the Spirit of the Rhine:

- Capture the spirit of the Rhine River in your farewell, embracing the sense of adventure and discovery.

- Convey the lasting impact this journey has had on your spirit.

Closing with Positivity:

- Close your farewell with positive sentiments, expressing appreciation for the entire Rhine River experience.

- End with well-wishes for future travels and the hope that the memories will forever linger in your heart.

Whether shared in person, in a farewell toast, or through a heartfelt note, your farewell on the Rhine River is an opportunity to encapsulate the essence of this extraordinary adventure and convey your deep appreciation for the moments that will remain etched in your travel tapestry.

APPENDIX

Language Tips: Basic German Phrases

Learning a few basic German phrases can enhance your travel experience along the Rhine River, where German is commonly spoken. Here are some useful phrases to help you communicate with locals:

Hello / Hi:

- German: Hallo

Goodbye:

- German: Auf Wiedersehen (formal) / Tschüss (informal)

Please:

- German: Bitte

Thank you:

- German: Danke

Excuse me / Sorry:

- German: Entschuldigung

Yes:

- German: Ja

No:

   - German: Nein

I don't understand:

   - German: Ich verstehe nicht

Can you help me, please?:

   - German: Können Sie mir bitte helfen?

Where is...?:

   - German: Wo ist...?

How much does this cost?:

   - German: Wie viel kostet das?

I would like...:

   - German: Ich hätte gerne...

Do you speak English?:

   - German: Sprechen Sie Englisch?

My name is...:

   - German: Ich heiße...

I'm lost:

- German: Ich habe mich verirrt

Cheers!:

- German: Prost!

Help!:

- German: Hilfe!

Bathroom / Toilet:

- German: Badezimmer / Toilette

Good morning:

- German: Guten Morgen

Good evening:

- German: Guten Abend

Remember to use a polite and friendly tone when communicating, and don't hesitate to try these phrases even if your German pronunciation isn't perfect. Locals often appreciate the effort, and it can lead to more enjoyable interactions during your Rhine River journey.

Made in the USA
Monee, IL
08 August 2024